Oregon Road Trips

Southwest Edition

Mike & Kristy Westby

Copyright © 2019 Mike & Kristy Westby

All rights reserved.

No part of this publication may be reproduced, distributed, linked to or transmitted in any form or by any means, including photocopying, recording or other electronic or mechanical methods, without the prior written permission of the publisher, except for brief quotations embodied in critical reviews and certain noncommercial uses permitted by copyright law.

No part of this publication may be made available for downloading online without the permission of Mike & Kristy Westby.

Although every precaution has been taken to verify the accuracy of the information contained herein, no responsibility is assumed for any errors or omissions, and no liability is assumed for damages that may result from the use of this information.

Active, Oregon™

Discover Scenic Backroads & Byways by Day,
Stay in Historic Hotels by Night™

ISBN-13: 978-0998395029

62719 - ING

Cover design by Sarah Craig – SarahCookDesign.com

"And above all, watch with glittering eyes the whole world around you, because the greatest secrets are always hidden in the most unlikely places."

Roald Dahl

FOLLOW DISCOVER-OREGON

Oregon's Crater Lake National Park at Sunrise

On the Web:
www.Discover-Oregon.com

On Twitter:
@DiscoverOre.com

On Facebook:
www.Facebook.com/DiscoverORE

On Instagram:
DiscoverOregon4300

OREGON ROAD TRIPS
SOUTHWEST EDITION

Discover Southwest Oregon!

An exciting 9-day vacation exploring Southwest Oregon's scenic backroads & byways is now as easy as 1-2-3...

1) Write in the Dates of Your Trip
2) Make Your Historic Hotel Reservations
3) Pack Your Bags and Go!

Using this easy-to-use guide, you'll simply turn each page as you motor along and choose which points of interest to stop at and explore during your day's journey, *all while making your way towards that evening's lodging at a historic Oregon hotel.*

An exciting vacation awaits...and it's already planned for you!

Your Journey

Introduction	Pg. 8
How To Begin	Pg. 9
Make Your Reservations	Pg. 11
Day 1 – To Crater Lake	Pg. 22
Day 2 – To Ashland	Pg. 42
Day 3 – To Jacksonville	Pg. 62
Day 4 – Explore Jacksonville	Pg. 76
Day 5 – To Idleyld Park	Pg. 92
Day 6 – To Grants Pass	Pg. 106
Day 7 – To the Oregon Caves NM	Pg. 126
Day 8 – Jetboat the Rogue River	Pg. 140
Day 9 – Going Home	Pg. 148
Helpful Phone Numbers	Pg. 150
About the Authors	Pg. 159

Introduction

Oregon's 11,240' Mt. Hood

Oregon is a vast and beautiful state. I could list its square mileage, its demographics or perhaps the distance from border to border, but a better description is...it starts with the shores of the Pacific Ocean on its western edge, traverses east over the Oregon Coast Range and into the verdant Willamette Valley, climbs over the snowy summits of the Cascade mountain range while skirting south of the sublime Columbia River Gorge and then continues forever into the remote, silent and dramatic beauty and history of eastern Oregon.

This guide is about setting out on your own adventure to explore Oregon. It's about the journey, not the destination. It's about asking, "I wonder what that is?" It's about hitting the brakes and turning left off the pavement. Opening a door and saying "Hello". Shutting off the engine, getting out of the car and listening to the silence of distance. It's about the angry tug on a fly line, wondering just how many stars a sky can hold and what would really happen, I mean *really* happen, if you just kept going.

Recently, my wife, Kristy, and I set out on a 9-day 959 mile journey along the backroads and byways of Southwest Oregon to discover its intriguing sites, small towns and scenic wonders, all while staying in historic hotels each evening. Our goal was to stop and explore all of the places we normally rush past when we're traveling, because we're in such a hurry to reach our destination. As we met folks along the way, we were surprised by how many said they've always wanted to make a similar trip but they didn't know where or how to begin planning it, and this was usually followed by a request for a copy of our itinerary and notes once we finished our journey. We decided to go one step further and write up our notes, add some photos, include some maps and turn it all into an easy-to-use book so that others could duplicate our trip with little effort, all while customizing it to their own interests and sense of adventure.

How To Begin

Oregon's immense size, historical treasures and abundance of geographical features are too much to capture in one trip. In fact, its countless riches can be so intimidating that travelers don't know where to begin...so they don't. Analysis paralysis.

Good news! This book already has your route planned for you. All you need to do is three simple things...

1) Select the 9-day period for your trip and write those dates into this book at the beginning of each chapter.

2) Call and make reservations at the historic hotels found at the end of each day, which correspond with your chosen dates.

3) Pack your bags, hop in the car and simply choose the sights you wish to stop at and explore each day as you motor along.

Note that some of the optional activities you'll enjoy during your trip, such as seeing a play in Ashland or jetboating the scenic Rogue River, will also require reservations, and these are noted at the beginning of each chapter/day.

WHERE TO START

The "official" first stop of your 9-day road trip is in Cottage Grove, Oregon, just south of Eugene, OR. We recommend you travel to Eugene the day before you begin and stay the night at the historic Campbell House Inn & Restaurant. See Page 19 for additional details.

ADD OR REMOVE A DAY TO CUSTOMIZE YOUR TRIP

While we have laid out a pre-planned 9-day road trip for you, with a little ingenuity, you can actually make this trip any length you choose. Feel free to begin your trip on perhaps Day 4 to shorten your journey, or add an extra night's stay or two along the way to lengthen it. (We highly recommend this for your stay in Jacksonville to see the wine country, or Ashland so as to enjoy a play.)

TIMING

Your Southwest Oregon road trip is a beautiful journey any time of the year, with the landscape changing dramatically from season to season. Note, however, that timing plays an important role early in the year. Travelers beginning a little before Memorial Day Weekend will be rewarded with lush green foliage and cascading waterfalls, yet many of the attractions along the way will be closed, since they wait until Memorial Day Weekend to open.

www.Discover-Oregon.com

MAKE YOUR RESERVATIONS

Historic Ashland Springs Hotel – Ashland, OR

These are the reservations you will need to make for your trip. All necessary lodging reservations are shown in bold. All others are optional activities.

Night 1 – Stay at The Campbell House Inn

- **Campbell House Inn - 503-541-343-1119**

Day 1 – Eugene, OR to Crater Lake Nat'l Park

Make a reservation for 1 night

- **Crater Lake Lodge – 541-594-2255**
- Crater Lake Trolley - 541-882-1896
- Crater Lake Boat Tours – 888-774-2728 (2 or more days in advance) or 24 hours in advance at self-service kiosks in the Crater Lake Lodge and the Annie Creek Gift Shop at Mazama Village.

Day 2 - Crater Lake Nat'l Park to Ashland, OR

Make a reservation for 1 night

- **Historic Ashland Springs Hotel - 541-488-1700**
- Any plays you wish to see - Visit: www.osfashland.org - See page 59 for additional details.

Day 3 - Ashland, OR to Jacksonville, OR

Make reservations for 2 nights

- **Jacksonville Inn - 541-899-1900**
- Harry & David Tour in Medford, OR - 877-322-8000
    - Reservations are not required, but there may be a wait during the busy seasons.

Day 4 - Explore Jacksonville, OR

Spend a second night at the Jacksonville Inn

- The Jacksonville Trolley - 541-899-8118
- Segway Tours of Jacksonville: 541-899-5269

Day 5 - Jacksonville, OR to Idleyld, OR

Make a reservation for 1 night

- **Steamboat Inn - 541-498-2230**

Day 6 - Idleyld, OR to Grants Pass, OR

Make reservations for night 6 and possibly night 8.
    - See page 148 before making your reservations here

- **The Weasku Inn - 541-471-8000**

Day 7 - Grants Pass, OR to the Oregon Caves NM

Make a reservation for 1 night

- **The Chateau at the Oregon Caves - 541-592-3400**
- Oregon Cave Tours - Recreation.gov - 877-444-6777

Day 8 - Oregon Caves NM back to Grants Pass, OR / The Rogue River

Make a reservation for 1 night if you're not driving home. This reservation is dependent upon what you reserved for Day / Night 6 at The Weasku Inn. See page 148 for additional details.

- **The Weasku Inn - 541-471-8000**
  or
- **The Lodge at Riverside - 5441-955-0600**
  or
- **The Wolf Creek Inn and Tavern** - Via Reserve America - 800-452-5687
- Rogue River Hellgate Jetboat Excursions - 541-479-7204 - See page 143 for jetboat excursion times.

Day 9 - Heading Home

www.Discover-Oregon.com

SOME GROUND RULES

"It's the Journey, Not the Destination."

The key to your journey is to alter your driving mindset. It really isn't about getting *there*, it's about discovering *here*. With this in mind, here are some ground rules to follow...

- Get used to stopping the car and getting out.
- Now stop the car and get out.
- Stop the car and get out...again. You'll be glad you did.
- Always ask "I wonder where that goes?"...and go there.
- Hit the brakes and turn left.
- Open the door and say "Hello."
- Don't assume it has to be a short conversation.
- Never mind that you just stopped back there...stop again here.
- Yes, it is a nice view. Feel free to stop, get out and admire it.
- This very moment is the time to do it. You won't be coming back this way next week.
- Enjoy the journey!

Travel Beyond the Page

By all means, do not feel you have to stop at only the places found in this book, as there are many more than those listed here just waiting to be discovered. Go ahead...follow that dusty road, stop at that small museum, walk the trail to the viewpoint, and open the door to the shop that looks closed, but isn't. It's all about taking the time to...discover Oregon.

The Same, But Different

Following the information in this guide, you will enjoy a unique and exciting vacation discovering Southwest Oregon. It's important to note, however, that with a little creativity, you can also make this same journey a second or third time and have it be an almost entirely new and different trip each time. With trip number one, you may find you have only enough time in your day to explore Crater Lake National Park, the Beekman Bank and Toketee Falls, leaving the Douglas County Museum, Oregon Caves National Monument and Hellgate Jetboat Excursions completely undiscovered. That means they'll all be waiting when you make your next trip.

Feel Free to Add a Day or Two

Keep in mind as you book your reservations that you can extend your road trip by simply booking a hotel reservation for two nights instead of one. This way, you'll have more time to explore the local area, catch a play, visit some wineries, hike a nearby trail and enjoy a leisurely dinner.

"So, Where Are You From?"

There are many blessings on a trip like this, one of which is the number of conversations you simply fall into. It usually begins with a simple question or comment, and the next thing you know, you're involved in a 30-minute conversation with some of the nicest people you've ever met. Why? Because the folks you meet on a trip like this are your neighbors, it's just that they're a quite a few houses further down the block. If you approach a town, café, museum or someone with an air of traveling arrogance, then you're making a huge mistake. Instead, be genuine and friendly. You'll be amazed at how many people you'll meet and how pleasant your trip will be.

And in those rare instances where you meet someone who loves to talk...about themselves...then excuse yourselves with the tried and true "Well, we need to be hitting the road if we're going to stay on schedule."

The Right Frame of Mind

During your journey, your mindset will make all the difference between having an amazing trip filled with fond memories that will last a lifetime or a less-than-stellar odyssey you'd just as soon forget. Is the single-pane window in your 1920s era hotel room a bit drafty? Then it's historically accurate, not in need of replacement. Did you come out to your car one morning only to discover a flat tire? Find a helpful Les Schwab Tire Store and be thankful it's not a broken spoke on a wagon wheel. Did the Beekman House close early because business was kind of slow today? Then that's exactly a taste of the slower pace of life you were seeking. Always go with the flow, and you'll be happy you did.

Get Some Good *Paper* Maps

We can't emphasize this enough. You will want to travel with and use a couple of good paper maps, and the more detailed, the better. Your phone will no doubt work well, but you're setting out to explore some remote parts of Southwest Oregon, many of which have no cell signal whatsoever, so your phone will not work there. In addition, your paper maps will always boot up and never run out of power.

As you make your way along and stop at various locations, you'll often see folded Oregon maps made available for free by the Oregon Department of Transportation. These are very helpful, so grab more than one and keep them with you at all times. For more detail on the backroads you'll be traveling, we also recommend the large Oregon atlases put out by DeLorme. You can find them online for about $25.

Oregon's tourism division, Travel Oregon, also issues very helpful maps, magazines and trip guides. We highly recommend you visit their web site, www.TravelOregon.com, to order some of these free guides before setting out on your trip. Especially helpful is their large *Oregon Scenic Byways Official Driving Guide*.

If you are a member of AAA, check their resources, as well. By the way, make sure your membership is up-to-date.

The Time of Year Makes a Difference

Your Discover Oregon journey is a trip best made during mid-spring to late fall, when temperatures are warm, the days are longer and the higher elevation roads are clear of snow and winter debris. Most roads are open year-round, but portions of the higher elevation roads, such as Cedar Flat Road out of Williams, OR, are closed due to snow in the early spring. Plan on most routes being snow free sometime in mid- to late May, though this can vary. If you're traveling during this time, call the corresponding Ranger Stations to get the latest road status. Travel tools, such as a small shovel and bow saw, may come in handy on a couple of routes, such as the road from Williams, OR to Selma, OR when traveling early in the year.

Note that many tourist related businesses and attractions open for the summer season beginning with Memorial Day Weekend at the end of May. Make this trip even one week earlier and you may find quite a few attractions are closed.

Be Prepared

Be self-sufficient as you travel along, as some areas are remote. Be sure to bring extra food, drinks, a first-aid kit, a roadside emergency kit, a phone charger with cables, a tire inflator, (yes, I've had to use one!) a blanket, maps, a small shovel, flashlights with fresh batteries, a lighter, a whistle, road flares and a small tarp to sit upon should you have to change a tire or dig out from some snow. Note that should you experience some kind of difficulties while on the road, chances are someone will be along soon.

Six Hours Per Day – Your Results May Vary

As we've said, it's all about the journey and not the destination. That said, we found that after about six hours of being on the road, we were flipping this mantra and were ready to reach our destination. Our willingness to stop and explore was being replaced by a desire to simply reach our hotel, relax and "be there." Everybody's results will certainly vary, but we found that about six hours on the road was enough for a day.

We'd Love to Hear About Your Trip!

It's one thing to spend months in front of a computer screen doing research, writing and turning all of this into a book, but it's an entirely different experience to hear from real people "out in the field" discovering Oregon. What kind of fun are you having? Where did you go? What did you like best? What did you not like at all? What do you think we should add to the book? Do not hesitate to send us a note or a photo of your adventures at ContactUs@Discover-Oregon.com. We'd love to hear from you!

www.Discover-Oregon.com

AN EARLY START IN EUGENE?

The first morning of your 9-day road trip begins with a drive along the scenic Cottage Grove Covered Bridge Tour Route, just south of Eugene, Oregon, where you'll enjoy discovering one historical covered bridge after another, as well as the fascinating Oregon Aviation Historical Museum near Cottage Grove, before making your way towards the stunning Crater Lake National Park.

To add a fun start to your road trip, you may want to consider staying at the Campbell House Inn & Restaurant in Eugene the night before you begin. By doing so, you can wake up the next morning, enjoy a casual breakfast at the Inn, and then begin Day 1.

Built in 1892 and fully restored as a historic boutique hotel, this quaint inn, located two hours south of the Portland Metro area, welcomes guests with luxuriously appointed rooms, beautifully landscaped grounds and a relaxing atmosphere.

>The Campbell House Inn & Restaurant
>252 Pearl Street
>Eugene, OR 97401
>541-343-1119

Note: If you begin your trip with an evening at the Campbell House Inn & Restaurant, you may also wish to consider arriving early enough in the day to explore some highlights of the Eugene area, including the Shelton McMurphey Johnson House, which is within walking distance from the Campbell House Inn, the nearby 5th Street Market with its collection of unique shops and restaurants, and the Lane County Historical Museum.

- Shelton McMurphey Johnson House
  303 Willamette Street
  Eugene, OR 97401
  541-484-0808
  10:00 a.m. - 1:00 p.m.
  Tuesday through Friday - $6.00

- 5th Street Market
  296 East 5th Ave. #300
  Eugene, OR 97401
  541-484-0383
  10:00 a.m. - 8:00 p.m.
  Monday through Saturday

- Lane County Historical Museum
  740 W 13th Ave.
  Eugene, OR 97402
  541-682-4242
  10:00 a.m. - 4:00 p.m.
  Tuesday through Saturday

Day One

Eugene, Oregon to Crater Lake National Park

Day 1
Eugene, OR to
Crater Lake National Park

Day 1 – Date: /   /

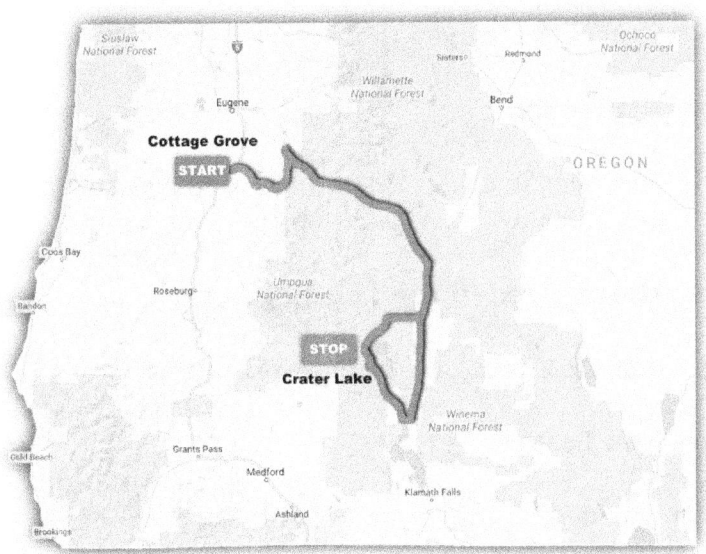

Summary: Where You're Going Today:

- Eugene, OR
- Cottage Grove, OR
- Cottage Grove Covered Bridge Tour Route
- Westfir, OR
- Oakridge, OR
- Crater Lake National Park

Your 9-Day Southwest Oregon road trip begins with a tour of some of Oregon's best-known covered bridges along the Cottage Grove Covered Bridge Tour Route. Along the way, you'll discover some of Oregon's rich aviation history, traverse an adventurous Forest Service road, discover Oregon's second highest single-drop waterfall, and pass through some beautiful southern Oregon scenery before making your way along the Volcanic Legacy Scenic Byway to Crater Lake, Oregon's only National Park.

Note: We recommend you don't get a late start today.

Tonight's Lodging:

- Crater Lake Lodge – Crater Lake National Park

Today's Mileage:

- 208 Miles to Crater Lake Lodge via the North Entrance
- 248 Miles to Crater Lake Lodge via the South Entrance

Reservations Needed for This Segment:

- Historic Crater Lake Lodge – 541-594-2255

Before You Leave:

Fill your gas tank in Eugene or Cottage Grove.

Start

Your "official" start of your trip begins south of Eugene, in Cottage Grove, where you'll drive into...and through...Oregon history along the Cottage Grove Covered Bridge Tour Route. Beginning with the large Chambers Bridge, the only covered railroad bridge west of the Mississippi, you'll embark on a tour in which you'll discover one quaint and historic covered bridge after another, often in a bucolic setting.

Note: If you are beginning your road trip early in the season and the north entrance to Crater Lake, off Hwy 138, is still closed due to snow, then you'll need to access Crater Lake Lodge at the end of today via the south entrance to the National Park, off Hwy 62. While this is a beautiful drive, it will require an extra 45 minutes to 1 hour of driving time, so plan your day accordingly. To get the latest status of both the north and south entrances to Crater Lake National Park call 541-594-3000.

☐ **First Stop:** Chambers Railroad Bridge

Built in 1925 to accommodate large steam engines pulling railcars with massive loads of timber, the Chambers Railroad Bridge is the only remaining covered railroad bridge in Oregon, as well as west of the Mississippi river. You'll find an interpretive display after walking through the bridge, which explains the bridge's history and the impressive restoration effort which returned it to its former glory.

> Chambers Railroad Bridge
> 1231 S. River Road
> Cottage Grove, OR 97424

Driving Directions: From I-5, take Exit 174 for Cottage Grove, OR. After the exit, turn right / west onto East Cottage Grove Con and follow this a short distance to N 9th Street. Proceed left / south onto N 9th Street and then turn right / west in ¼ mile onto W Woodson Pl. Shortly thereafter, turn left / south onto N River Rd. and follow this a little over 1 mile to the Chambers Railroad Bridge, which will be on your left.

☐ **Next Stop:** Centennial Covered Bridge and Veteran's Memorial

Built from the timbers of the 1922 Meadows and 1948 Brumbaugh covered bridges, the Centennial Covered Bridge serves today as a pedestrian and bike bridge, and more importantly, as part of a Veteran's memorial.

Driving Directions: Return north on S River Road for .68 miles and find the Centennial Covered Bridge and Veteran's Memorial in Riverside Park, across E Main Street.

☐ **Next Stop:** Oregon Aviation Historical Society

One of our favorite things about our Oregon road trips is opening a door and being unsure or even hesitant about what we'll find inside, and then leaving and thinking "That was a great find!" The Oregon Aviation Historical Society museum fits that description. With its non-descript metal exterior and single small door for an entrance, it gives the impression there isn't much inside, but open the door and you'll find the Oregon Aviator's Hall of Fame backed by an impressive ever-growing collection of colorful antique hand-built aircraft. Check in at the office at the end of the hallway and inquire about a tour.

Oregon Aviation Historical Society
2475 Jim Wright Way
Cottage Grove, OR 97424

Driving Directions: Returning the way you came, drive north on N River Road. Turn right / east onto W Woodson Place, and then left / northwest onto N 9th Street. In ¼ mile, veer right / west onto E Cottage Grove Con and follow this under I-5 as it becomes Row River Road. In ¼ mile from I-5, turn left / north onto Jim Wright Way and you'll see the Oregon Aviation Historical Society building on your right.

☐ **Next Stop:** Currin Covered Bridge

A few of the 13 covered bridges you'll see today and throughout your Southwest Oregon road trip have characteristics which make them unique. The Chambers Railroad Bridge, which you saw earlier today, is the only covered railroad bridge west of the Mississippi, the Office Bridge is the only bridge which contains a covered pedestrian walkway, and in the case of the 1925 Currin Bridge, it is the only bridge in Oregon with a main body painted in two different colors; red for the sides and white for the portals.

Currin Covered Bridge
Layng Road
Cottage Grove, OR 97424

Driving Directions: Return to Row River Road and turn left / east. Follow this for 2.8 miles to Layng Road. Turn right / south onto Layng Road and find the Currin Covered Bridge on your right.

☐ **Next Stop:** Mosby Creek Covered Bridge

While the 1920 Mosby Creek Covered Bridge is the oldest covered bridge in Lane County, it is one of the few covered bridges in the area which still handles traffic. Parking is limited, but there is a small pullout on the east end, just beyond the guard rail.

Mosby Creek Covered Bridge
77935 Layng Rd.
Cottage Grove, OR 97424

Driving Directions: From the Currin Covered Bridge, continue south on Layng Road for 1.2 miles to the Mosby Creek bridge.

☐ **Next Stop:** Stewart Covered Bridge

Closed to vehicular traffic, the quaint 1930 Stewart Covered Bridge is today preserved as part of an Oregon Scenic Bikeway.

Driving Directions: From the Mosby Creek Covered Bridge, continue south on Layng Road to Mosby Creek Road. Turn left here and follow this 1.2 miles southeast to Garoutte Rd. Turn left / east onto Garoutte Road and you'll find the Stewart Covered Bridge on your left.

☐ Next Stop: Dorena Covered Bridge

At 105 feet in length, the 1949 Dorena Covered Bridge is one of the larger bridges you'll see today. Inside, you'll find huge wooden trusses supporting its sizeable exterior, which is adorned with distinctive louvered windows looking out on the Row River below. While  the bridge is bypassed by a newer concrete span nearby, you can still drive across it to a small parking area on its far end.

 Directions - From the Mosby Creek bridge, continue west on Garoutte Road approximately 2.5 miles to Shoreview Drive / Government Road. Turn left / northwest here and follow this 1.1 miles to Row River Road. Turn right / north here and follow Row River Road for a little over 7 miles as it makes its way along Dorena Lake, where you'll then reconnect with Shoreview Drive. You'll see the Dorena Covered Bridge from this intersection. Turn right, cross the river, and then turn left. Drive through the Dorena Covered Bridge to find parking on its far side.

☐ Next Stop: Willamette Highway / Highway 58

Your next "destination" is the Willamette Highway, also known as Highway 58. This will take you east to Hwy 97, which in turn will lead you to this evening's lodging at Crater Lake.

To get "there" from "here" will require a bit of adventure as you traverse 18.3 miles along a remote gravel road through the mountains. Note that there is no cell service along this route.

Directions:

- From the Dorena Covered Bridge, turn right / east onto Shoreview Drive / Government Road, which immediately turns into Row River Road. Follow Row River Road for 7.83 miles to the gravel road turnoff on the left for Layng Creek Road / NF-17, just west of the small town of Disston. You'll see a large sign here with directions to Layng Creek Rd., Rujada Campground, State Highway 58, and Holland Point Junction.

- Reset your odometer at this turnoff.

- Follow Layng Creek Road / NF-17 and stay left on NF-17 at the sharp bend, which occurs at 8.73 miles.

- Turn left onto NF-5840 at approximately 13.6 miles.

- Follow this to Hwy 58 at approximately 18.3 miles.

Important: This remote gravel road is well-maintained during the Spring, Summer and Fall months, and it typically remains "open" and passable in the winter, but may at times be blocked due to snow or winter debris on the road. If there is any snow on the road, do not continue, but instead return west via Row River Road to Cottage Grove, take I-5 north to just south of Eugene, OR, and gain access to Hwy 58 there.

For current road conditions for Layng Creek Road / NF-17 and NF-5840, contact the **Cottage Grove Ranger District office at 541-767-5000**.

☐ **Next Stop:** Lowell Covered Bridge - Optional

This next stop is optional, as it involves a bit of a detour back west along Hwy 58 to the town of Lowell. The payoff, however, is another historic covered bridge, the widest in all of Oregon.

Originally built in 1907 and rebuilt in 1945, the Lowell Covered Bridge was designed and built by Nes Roney, a bridge builder who built many of Oregon's early covered bridges, as well as the Shelton McMurphey Johnson House in Eugene, which is near the historic Campbell House, the optional first night's "pre-trip" stay we recommend in this book on Page 19.

Driving Directions: From where you connect with Hwy 58 from NF-5840, turn left / west and proceed for 11.5 miles to South Pioneer Street at Lowell, OR. Turn right / north here and you will immediately find the bridge. Drive to the far end to find a large parking area, complete with an interpretive kiosk.

☐ **Next Stop:** Office Covered Bridge - Oakridge Oregon

In addition to being Oregon's longest covered bridge at 180', the large red Office Covered Bridge is also the only covered bridge west of the Mississippi River which has a separate pedestrian walkway incorporated into the bridge design.

Built in 1941 and rebuilt in 1944 after a flood, the Office Covered Bridge is so named because it was built by the Westfir Lumber Company to allow logging trucks to carry heavy loads of timber to the company's sawmill located on the west side of the bridge, which is now a parking area and trailhead. (Take note of the large timbers and extra beams used inside the bridge to support the weight of the trucks.) The "office", or headquarters, for the Westfir Lumber Company was located in what is now the Westfir Lodge, which is found today at the east end of the bridge.

Office Covered Bridge
Westfir, OR 97492

Driving Directions: From the Lowell Covered Bridge, return to Hwy 58. From the intersection with Hwy 58, turn left / east and follow Hwy 58 for 18.2 miles to Westfir Road, opposite the large Forest Service office building. (Look for the large sign for Westfir, OR here) Turn left / west onto Westfir Road and follow this approximately ½ mile, where you'll turn left / north while continuing on Westfir Road. Follow this 1¾ miles to the town of Westfir and the Office Bridge. Drive through the bridge and park in the large parking area on the opposite side. Interpretive signs and restrooms can be found here.

☐ **Next Stop:** The Westfir Lodge

Located next to the Office Bridge and in the heart of some of the finest mountain biking, road cycling, fly fishing, and skiing in the state, the historic 1925 Westfir Lodge offers accommodations designed specifically with the outdoor enthusiast in mind.

Nine rooms with outdoor or historic theming welcome guests after each day of adventure, and a large living room is perfect for sharing a glass of wine with friends while telling tales of fish caught, trails traveled and single-track explored. Take a moment after dinner to visit the room which is a recreation of one of the original 1920s era lumber mill offices which used to make up the lodge.

The Westfir Lodge
47365 1st Street
Westfir, OR 97492
541-782-3103

Driving Directions: The Westfir Lodge can be found at the east end of the Office Bridge.

☐ **Next Stop:** Salt Creek Falls

A quick detour off of Hwy 58, followed by a short walk, brings you to the beautiful Salt Creek Falls. Oregon's second highest single drop waterfall, it plunges 286 feet from its crest to a deep pool below before continuing through a mossy forested valley.

Driving Directions: From the Office Bridge, return to Hwy 58 via the route you came. Turn left / east onto Hwy 58 and follow this for 25.6 miles to NF-5893 for the Salt Creek Summit Sno-Park. Turn right / south off of Hwy 58 onto NF-5893 and follow the road a short distance back west to the falls parking area. Note: This parking area requires a $5 Day Use fee or a Northwest Forest Pass.

www.Discover-Oregon.com

☐ **Next Stop:** Odell Lake / Odell Lake Lodge & Resort

Stop in at Odell Lake Lodge & Resort to get a sense of the classic small lodges and resorts which can be found at numerous alpine lakes throughout Oregon. Breakfast, lunch and dinner are available indoors, as well as outside on the patio.

Odell Lake Lodge & Resort
21501 NF-680
Crescent, OR 97733
541-433-2540

Driving Directions: From Salt Creek Falls, return to Hwy 58 and continue 10.3 miles to E Odell Lake Road, at the east end of Odell Lake. Turn right / south onto E Odell Lake Road and follow this to Odell Lake Lodge & Resort.

Note: Your next stop is at Collier State Park, and then Crater Lake National Park. There is no gas available within all of Crater Lake National Park, and gas stations are limited as you begin to approach the park, so be sure you have fuel before you arrive. You will find a gas station in Chemult, OR, 8.4 miles after connecting with Hwy 97 South from Hwy 58 and prior to reaching Hwy 138, which leads to the north entrance to Crater Lake NP. There is also gas available at Sand Creek Station, south of Hwy 138 for those driving to the south entrance.

Sand Creek Station
71810 Hwy 97 North, Sand Creek Rd.
Chiloquin, OR 97624
541-365-4439

■ **Next Stop:** Collier State Park Logging Museum

If you are not accessing Crater Lake National Park via the north entrance off of Hwy 138, but instead having to continue southward to access it via its south entrance due to Hwy 138 being closed for the winter, then you'll pass the Collier State Park Logging Museum on Hwy 97 along the way. Expertly curated by volunteers, this outdoor museum presents rare logging equipment and artifacts, a Pioneer village, interpretive displays showcasing the turn-of-the-20th-century technological advancements in logging, and more.

> Collier State Park Logging Museum
> 46000 Hwy 97
> Chiloquin, OR 97624
> 541-783-2471

Open: The museum is open from 8:00 a.m. to 8:00 p.m., June through August – 8:00 a.m. to 4:00 p.m., September through May. The Day Use area is open year-round.

Driving Directions: From Odell Lake Lodge & Resort, return to Hwy 58 and turn right / east. Follow Hwy 58 for 18.5 miles and then merge onto Hwy 97 south. Proceed south for approximately 49 miles to the large sign for the Collier Logging Museum, which is on your right.

Photo © Gary Halvorson – Oregon State Archives

www.Discover-Oregon.com

Tonight's Lodging - Crater Lake Lodge - Crater Lake National Park

Photo © NPS.gov

Tonight's lodging is at the historic Crater Lake Lodge, a rare opportunity to stay overnight in one of America's beautiful National Parks.

Built in 1915, the recently refurbished yet rustic Crater Lake Lodge sits on the southwest rim of Crater Lake, with many of its 71 rooms offering stunning views of the lake's vibrant blue waters shimmering over 1,000' below. Surrounding the lake is the never-ending caldera wall, reaching 2,000' high in some places and offering a sense of the violent volcanic past which gave

life to the lake. Inside, visitors will find an authentic northwest atmosphere, with a great room just off the lobby offering cozy reading spots, a large stone fireplace casting a warm glow, and walls lined with rugged bark from Pacific Northwest forests. Outside, guests can enjoy large wooden rocking chairs, which are lined up on the patio for taking in views of the lake in a lofty alpine setting.

The lodge's rooms have been refurbished, as well, and offer basic yet very pleasant accommodations, complete with private baths. East facing rooms provide an impressive view of the lake, as well as the morning sunrise.

Note: It is best to make your reservations far in advance (Up to 180 days) of your preferred arrival. If rooms are not available for the dates of your choice, be sure to check back on a regular basis to see if there have been any cancellations.

- Crater Lake Lodge Reservations: More than 2 days in advance – Call 888-774-2728

- Crater lake Lodge Reservations: For tonight and tomorrow night – Call 541-594-2255 – xt 3200

- Crater Lake Lodge Lodging Information: 541-594-3000

Note: While the road to Crater Lake Lodge is generally open year-round, depending upon snowfall, Crater Lake Lodge itself is only open from mid-May to mid-October.

For those who would like a unique souvenir, the dining plates you use while dining in the lodge's restaurant are available for sale. Inquire at the front desk in the lobby or with your waiter.

>Crater Lake Lodge
>565 Rim Drive
>Klamath Falls, OR 97604

Lodging Option: The Cabins at Mazama Village

Located amongst tall Ponderosa Pines only seven miles south of Rim Village and Crater Lake Lodge, The Cabins at Mazama Village make an excellent in-park second choice when rooms at Crater Lake Lodge are not available. Each cabin offers clean and basic accommodations, with one or two queen beds and a private bath with a shower. Microwaves, telephones and televisions are not available. A small store and café are a short stroll away. Lake views are not available here.

The Cabins at Mazama Village are located approximately 7 miles south of Crater Lake Lodge, on the main road leading in and out of the park. For additional directions, see "Approaching from the South" in the driving directions below.

>The Cabins at Mazama Village
>569 Mazama Village Drive
>Crater Lake, OR 97604
>541-594-2255

- Open late May to late September

- Crater Lake Lodge / Cabin Reservations: More than 2 days in advance – 888-774-2728

- Crater lake Lodge / Cabin Reservations: For tonight and tomorrow night – 541-594-2255 – xt 3200

- See more phone numbers for Crater Lake on Page 150

Driving Directions to Crater Lake Lodge

There are two approaches to Crater Lake and Crater Lake Lodge, one from the north (Hwy 138) and one from the south. (Hwy 62) The north entrance is open only during the months of June through October because of snow, whereas the south entrance is open year-round.

For current road conditions and to check if the north entrance is open, contact Crater Lake Park Dispatch at 541-594-3000. Dial 0 to speak with a Ranger. Note: There is a $10 National Park entrance fee, and this is valid for 7 days.

Approaching from the North

From the junction of Hwy 58 and Hwy 97, proceed south on Hwy 97 for 18 miles to the exit for Hwy 138. Turn right / west onto Hwy 138 / Volcanic Legacy Scenic Byway and continue approximately 15 miles to the turn off to Crater Lake National Park. Turn left / south onto Hwy 209 / North Entrance Road and proceed a short distance to the North Entrance Station. Pay a park entrance fee of $10 and proceed to Rim Village and Crater Lake Lodge.

Approaching from the South

From the junction of Hwy 58 and Hwy 97, proceed south on Hwy 97 for 52.5 miles (Passing the Collier State Park Logging Museum along the way) to Exit 247 for Hwy 422 / Chiloquin Hwy, which leads to Hwy 62. Turn right / west onto Hwy 422 and follow this 3 miles to where it meets with Hwy 62. Turn right / north onto Hwy 62 and continue 25 miles to Munson Valley Road, the turn for Crater Lake. Turn right / east and follow this to Rim Village and Crater Lake Lodge, as well as The Cabins at Mazama Village.

Notes

Day Two

Crater Lake to Ashland, OR

DAY 2
CRATER LAKE TO ASHLAND

Day 2 – Date: /   /

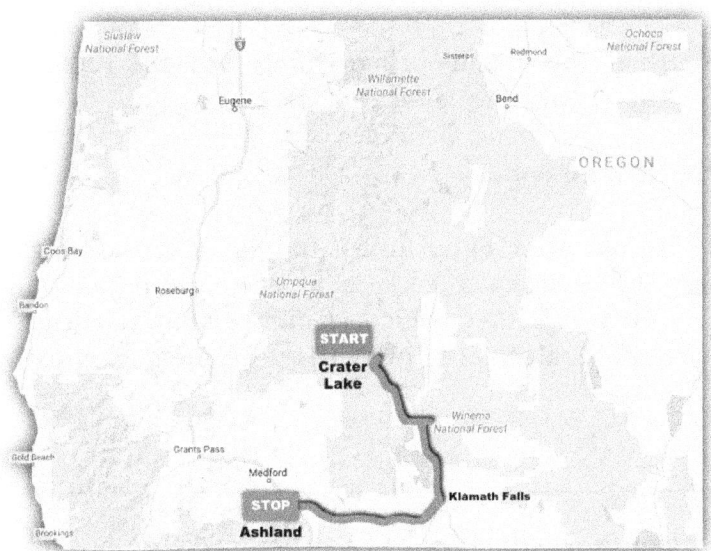

Summary: Where You're Going Today

- Crater Lake National Park
- Fort Klamath, OR
- Chiloquin, OR
- Klamath Falls, OR
- Ashland, OR

"The play's the thing!" It's also the destination, as today you leave Crater Lake National Park to explore an interesting bookstore, ride aboard a historic miniature railroad, take a scenic hike, visit a unique museum, and end up at the historic Ashland Springs Hotel in Ashland, OR, home of the annual Shakespeare Festival.

Tonight's Lodging:

- Historic Ashland Springs Hotel

Today's Mileage: 132 Miles

Reservations Needed for This Segment:

- Historic Ashland Springs Hotel - 541-488-1700
- Crater Lake Trolley - 541-882-1896

Before You Leave:

 Your first opportunity for gas after leaving Crater Lake National Park is at the Crater Lake Junction Travel Center, which is immediately north of where the Crater Lake Hwy / Hwy 62 merges with Hwy 97 southbound.

Start

Travel southeast from Crater Lake National Park on Hwy 62 to Hwy 97 South, which takes you to Klamath Falls. Enjoy the sights here before turning due west on the Green Springs Highway / Hwy 66, a scenic two lane backroad which winds its way towards your destination for the day, Ashland, OR.

☐ **Crater Lake Stop:** 33 Mile Rim Drive

 Part of Oregon's Volcanic Legacy Scenic Byway, the 33 mile drive around the rim of Crater Lake's caldera is an excellent way to get a full sense of this unique Oregon treasure. Multiple pullouts along the drive give plenty of opportunities to get out and

experience the grandeur of the lake from constantly changing viewpoints. Plan on 1.5 to 2.0 hours to complete the tour.

Driving Directions: The Rim Drive is a 33 mile loop. Drive south from Rim Village and Crater Lake Lodge on Munson Valley Road and turn left / east on the Rim Drive at 3 miles.

☐ **Crater Lake Stop:** The Crater Lake Trolley

Want to enjoy the 33 mile rim drive around Crater Lake and leave the driving to someone else so you can enjoy the view? Then make your reservations on the new Crater Lake Trolley. Carrying up to 25 passengers each, three historically designated trolleys  make a tour around the lake each day with several stops along the way at specific areas of interest. Each tour takes approximately 2 hours and includes a National Park guide / interpreter who not only provides information about the lake and its volcanic past, but is more than happy to answer any questions you may have. All of the trolleys are ADA compliant. Tickets may be purchased online or on-site. Learn more at CraterLakeTrolley.net

Reservations:

- CraterLakeTrolley.net
- 541-882-1896
- Hours: Monday through Sunday: 8:00 a.m. - 8:30 p.m.
- Open during spring, summer and fall months, weather and snow permitting.

Note: All trolley boarding occurs at the Crater Lake Community House, which is immediately west of the Rim Village Visitor Center, just northwest of Crater Lake Lodge.

☐ **Crater Lake Stop:** Crater Lake Boat Tours

A truly unique Oregon adventure.

Seeing Crater Lake from the crater rim is a highlight of your trip, but seeing it from water level aboard a boat is a rare Oregon experience and a memory you won't soon forget. Three tours are offered:

1) The Standard Volcano Cruise – Tour the lake while learning about its history, geology and cultural significance. Allow 2 hours for the cruise, plus up to 1.5 hours to drive and hike to the departure point, Cleetwood Cove. Six departures daily.

2) The Wizard Island Tour – Guests travel for 45 minutes to Wizard Island where they are dropped off for thee hours to explore, fish, swim and even hike to the summit for a rare perspective of the lake. When the boat returns, guests will then board and enjoy a 75 minute counter-clockwise interpretive tour of the lake.

3) The Wizard Island Shuttle – For those who want to explore Wizard Island for three hours but not take the time for a full lake tour afterwards. Includes morning and afternoon departures.

Note: Daily tours are weather permitting. Visit www.CraterLakeLodges.com for the latest scheduled departure times. Reservations may be made by phone, online and at self-service kiosks. 50% of the tickets are available for purchase at least 2 days in advance by calling 888-774-2728. The remaining 50% are available exactly 24 hours before any given tour at self-service kiosks located in the lobby of Crater Lake Lodge and the Annie Creek Gift Shop at Mazama Village.

All boats depart from Cleetwood Cove on the north shore of Crater Lake, which is up to 90 minutes away from Crater Lake Lodge and the Rim Village. The 1.1 mile trail to the cove makes its way from the rim down to the water while losing 700' in elevation and can take up to 45 minutes to descend and an hour or more to ascend afterwards.

For additional information about the tours, contact Crater Lake National Park at 541-594-3000.

Driving Directions: From Crater Lake Lodge, proceed north on Rim Drive, driving in a clockwise direction around the lake for 11 miles to the large parking area for Cleetwood Cove. Restrooms are available here. Allow additional time for slow traffic along the route.

☐ Crater Lake Stop: Cleetwood Cove Trail

For those who wish to hike to the shore of Crater Lake, there is the Cleetwood Cove Trail, the only trail which reaches the water's edge. Dropping 700' in elevation from the crater's rim, the south-facing well-maintained trail descends...and ascends on the  way back up...at a steep 11% grade, so hikers are encouraged to be fit, wear sturdy shoes and bring water. This trail is also used by guests using the tour boats on Crater Lake.

Driving Directions: From Crater Lake Lodge, proceed north on Rim Drive, driving in a clockwise direction around the lake for 11 miles to the large parking area for Cleetwood Cove. Note: The trail is typically covered in snow until June or July, depending up the previous winter's snowfall.

☐ **Crater Lake Stop:** Annie Creek Canyon

As you make your way south from Crater Lake Lodge and the Rim Village, you'll notice numerous large pullouts on your left as you drive through the forest. From these pullouts, you can walk a short distance to see the dramatic Annie Creek Canyon with its interesting geologic pinnacles and unique features.

Driving Directions: Drive south from Crater Lake Lodge on Munson Valley Road to Hwy 62 / Volcanic Legacy Scenic Byway. Turn left / south and proceed for 4.6 miles to the turnout for Annie Falls. As you continue south on Hwy 62, you'll find additional places to pull over and view Annie Creek Canyon.

☐ **Next Stop:** Fort Klamath Historic Cemetery

You'll pass many different cemeteries as you make your Southwest Oregon road trip, but few, if any, are in such a beautiful setting as the Fort Klamath Historic Cemetery.

Driving Directions: From the Annie Falls parking area, proceed south on Hwy 62 / Volcanic Legacy Scenic Byway for 12 miles, where you'll find the cemetery on the right.

www.Discover-Oregon.com

☐ **Next Stop**: Fort Klamath Frontier Military Post

Comprised of a collection of buildings from the 19th century, the Fort Klamath Frontier Military Post Museum is an 8-acre outdoor museum dedicated to preserving the story of this important piece of Southwest Oregon history. Established in 1863, it consisted of over 50 different buildings, including a jail, guard house, Post Office, sawmill and more, all of which ceased operation over 100 years ago, in 1890.

Fort Klamath Frontier Military Post
51400 Hwy 62
Fort Klamath, OR 97626
541-381-2230

- Open Monday – Sunday, 10:00 a.m. – 6:00 p.m.
- Memorial Day Weekend through Labor Day Weekend

Driving Directions: Proceed south on Hwy 62 from the Fort Klamath Historic Cemetery for approximately ½ mile.

☐ **Next Stop**: Chiloquin Books & Collectibles

Chiloquin Books & Collectibles is one of those fun Oregon attractions that has an exterior which belies what's inside. Walk through the front door and you'll find aisle after aisle stacked to the ceiling with books, over 250,000 of them in fact, all neatly arranged and categorized by topic. We left with some treasures in hand, all at a good price, and you will, too.

Chiloquin Books & Collectibles / Arts Center
414 West Chocktoot Street
Chiloquin, OR 97624
541-783-2022

Driving Directions: From the Fort Klamath Frontier Military Post, proceed south on Hwy 62 / Volcanic Legacy Scenic Byway for 6.9 miles to Hwy 422 / Chiloquin Hwy. Turn left / east and proceed 4.2 miles on Hwy 422, under Hwy 97, to the town of Chiloquin and the Chiloquin Books & Collectibles / Arts Center on your right.

☐ **Next Stop**: Train Mountain Railroad and Klamath & Western Railroad

From the Sumpter Valley Railway and the Condon, Kinzua and Southern Railroad, to the Klamath Lake Railroad and SP Tillamook Branch, railroads have been a big part of the history of Oregon and the west. This next stop is a rare opportunity to experience a taste of Oregon railroading history up close.

Located right next to each other southwest of Chiloquin, OR are two attractions dedicated to showcasing the history of railroads in Oregon, as well as the hobby of miniature steam railroading.

Train Mountain Railroad Museum

Featuring the world's largest miniature railroad with over 36 miles of track covering 2,200 acres, as well as the largest collection of cabooses in the world, all complemented by an impressive display of full-size antique "rolling stock", the Train Mountain Museum and Institute offers self-guided tours of its facility, as well as rides upon its miniature railroad.

Train Mountain Railroad Museum & Institute
36941 South Chiloquin Road
Chiloquin, OR 97624
541-783-3030

- Open year-round
- Summer Hours: Monday through Friday – 9:00 a.m. – 3:00 p.m.
- Winter Hours: Monday through Friday – 10:00 a.m. – 2:00 p.m.

Klamath & Western Railroad, Inc.

Located next door to the Train Mountain Museum & Institute is the Klamath & Western Railroad, offering free rides through the forest aboard its miniature trains. Lunch, beverages and snack items are available at the K&W Diner. There is no fee for this attraction, but donations are appreciated.

Klamath & Western Railroad, Inc.
36951 South Chiloquin Road
Chiloquin, OR 97624
541-783-3177

- Open Saturdays – 10:00 a.m. – 3:00 p.m. – Memorial Day weekend through Labor Day weekend

Driving Directions: From Chiloquin Books & Collectibles, return back north / northwest on Hwy 422 only a few hundred feet and turn left / southeast onto what is also Hwy 422, which now proceeds in a different direction than the Hwy 422 you used to get to Chiloquin. Continue southeast on Hwy 422 for 1 mile to Hwy 97. Cross Hwy 97 and continue on what is now S Chiloquin Road for less than one mile to your destination on the left.

☐ Next Stop: Klamath Falls

Your next stop is in the town of Klamath Falls, which is home to a number of interesting buildings and museums, which showcase the rich and varied history of the area. You may also choose to have lunch here, or at the Green Springs Inn a little further down the road on Hwy 66 / Green Springs Highway.

Driving Directions: From the Train Mountain Railroad and Klamath & Western Railroad, return to Hwy 97 and drive south for 23.5 miles to where Hwy 97 splits. Take the exit here for Weed / San Francisco and proceed 2.4 miles, exiting the highway at the exit ramp for the Favell Museum - Info Center. From the exit, turn right onto Main Street and proceed northeast into Klamath Falls.

☐ Klamath Falls Stop: Baldwin Hotel Museum

The 1911 Baldwin Hotel Museum presents 40 rooms curated with period-specific artifacts depicting the elements of everyday life in the Klamath Falls area during the turn of the 20th century.

One and two hour guided tours are available during operating hours. Typically, visitors can simply arrive and ask to take a tour, with one hour tours covering the first two floors, and the two hour tours covering all four. No reservations are required.

Baldwin Hotel Museum
31 Main Street
Klamath Falls, OR 97601
541-883-4207

- Open Memorial Day weekend through Labor Day weekend – 10:00 a.m. through 4:00 p.m., Wednesday through Saturday. The last tour of the day begins at 2:30 p.m.

Driving Directions: You'll find the Baldwin Hotel Museum on your left shortly after turning right onto Main Street from the highway exit.

☐ Klamath Falls Stop: Favell Museum

Depicting the life of Native Americans in Southern Oregon, the Columbia River Gorge and the coastal areas of North America prior to the arrival of the white man, this extensive collection features artifacts dating back over 12,000 years ago, including thousands of arrowheads, spear points, ancient stone tools, basketry, pottery and more.

Favell Museum
125 W Main Street
Klamath Falls, OR 97601
541-882-9996

- Open Tuesday – Saturday, 10:00 a.m. – 4:00 p.m.
- Admission: Adults: $10, Children 6 to 16: $5,

Driving Directions: From the Baldwin Hotel Museum, drive west on Main Street, under Hwy 97 and across the river, to find the museum on your right.

☐ **Klamath Falls Stop**: The Goeller House

Make your way to the west side of Klamath Falls and find The Goeller House, an amazing example of Queen Anne Victorian architecture, though now in need of extensive repair. Designed by George F. Barber and listed on the National Register of Historic Places, the home was built by John Goeller between 1900 and 1905 using components from a mail-order catalog, *The Cottage Souvenir Number Two: A Repository of Artistic Cottage Architecture and Miscellaneous Design*, the same catalog used with the beautiful Nunan home in Jacksonville, OR, which you will see on Day 4.

Note: The Goeller House is a private residence and is not open to the public.

> The Goeller House
> 234 Riverside Dr.
> Klamath Falls, OR 97601

Driving Directions: From the Favell Museum, proceed south on Riverside Drive, which is immediately south of the museum, for 0.2 miles to find the Goeller House on your right.

☐ **Klamath Falls Stop**: Klamath County Museum

In addition to serving as the main office for the Baldwin Hotel Museum and the Fort Klamath Frontier Military Post, the Klamath County Museum features exhibits on the fascinating natural and human history of the area. In addition, it presents a display on the incendiary and explosive balloon bombs deployed by the Japanese during WWII. One such bomb landed near Klamath Falls, just east of Bly, OR, resulting in the only deaths attributed to the Japanese on contiguous American soil during WWII.

Klamath County Museum
1451 Main Street
Klamath Falls, OR
541-883-4208

- Open year-round 9:00 a.m. - 5:00 p.m. - Tuesday through Saturday

Driving Directions: From the Goeller House, return east onto Main Street, and since it is one way, veer right onto Klamath Avenue. Follow this ¾ mile to S Broad Street and then turn left / north towards Main Street. In one block, turn right onto Main Street and you'll find the museum on your left.

☐ **Lunch Stop**: Lunch at the Green Springs Inn

In addition to a couple of lunch options in Klamath Falls, the restaurant at the Green Springs Inn & Cabins makes for a great place to have lunch before you enjoy the nearby Green Springs Mountain Loop hike. They serve American fare for breakfast, lunch and dinner, all in a forested Oregon lodge setting.

Green Springs Inn
11470 Highway 66
Ashland, OR 97520
541-890-6435

- Open Monday - Sunday: 9:00 a.m. - 8:30 p.m.

Note: Disguised as a rusty old gas pump, the Green Springs Inn has an electric charging station out front for all makes of electric automobiles, including hybrids.

Driving Directions: From the Klamath County Museum, return to Hwy 97 via Main Street. Proceed on Hwy 97 south for 1¾ miles to Exit 277 for Hwy 66 / Green Springs Highway, leading to Lakeview and Medford. Turn right from the exit and take Hwy 66 west for 41.2 miles to the Green Springs Inn.

☐ **Next Stop**: Green Springs Mountain Loop Hike

At only 2.2 miles in length and with little elevation gain, the Green Springs Mountain Loop is a popular hike, which rewards hikers with stunning scenic vistas over Southern Oregon valleys. During the spring and summer, months it also offers an abundance of colorful wildflowers, as well as occasional sightings of the rare small orange Mardon Skipper butterfly.

Driving Directions: From the Green Springs Inn, proceed west on Hwy 66 for 1¾ miles to Old Hyatt Prairie Road. Turn right / north onto Old Hyatt Prairie Road and follow the signs for the Green Springs Mountain Loop Trail 1.2 miles to the small trail head parking area.

Hiking Directions:

From the parking area, walk northwest for a few minutes on the gravel road you drove in on and look for the intersection with the Pacific Crest Trail. Here, you'll see a sign for Green Springs Mountain Loop Connector. Follow this trail as it makes its way westward around a small meadow and pass through a gate. Continue north into the forest as you make your way counterclockwise on the loop trail. Soon, you'll reach a three-way junction with the Pacific Crest Trail, complete with a sign that reads PCT South / PCT North / Green Springs Connector. Take the PCT South trail (left) and follow this past beautiful scenic vistas before turning north back towards your car, thus competing the loop. Note: If you take the PCT North trail at the three-way junction, you'll also see some beautiful vistas, but return to the junction and continue on PCT South.

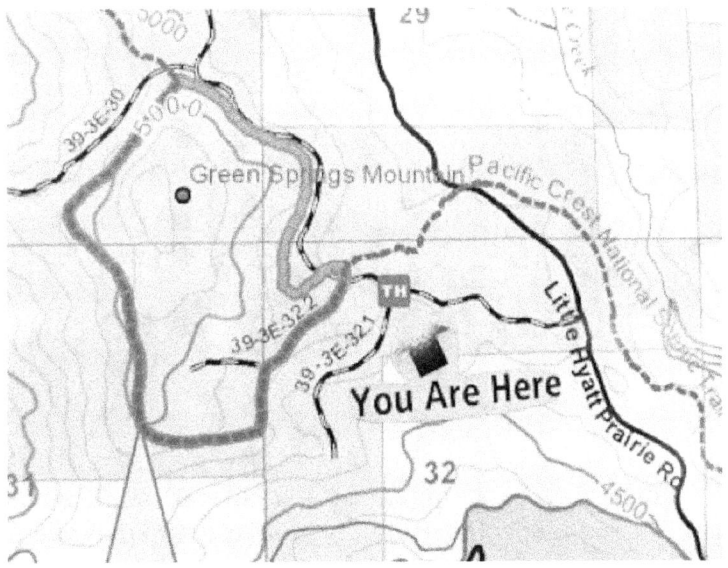

Image © TableRockTrekker.blogspot.com

www.Discover-Oregon.com

Tonight's Lodging - The Ashland Springs Hotel Ashland, OR

All the world may be a stage, but a small part of it is also the historic Ashland Springs Hotel. Popular with playgoers and attendees of the annual Shakespeare Festival, the 1925 Ashland Springs Hotel's grand lobby and 70 rooms welcome guests with a historic elegance complemented with modern day amenities.

Ashland Springs Hotel
212 E Main Street
Ashland, OR 97520
541-488-1700

Driving Directions: From the Green Springs Mountain Loop hike, return to Hwy 66 and turn right / west. Proceed for 16.3 miles as Hwy 66 descends and progresses into Ashland, OR, connecting with Hwy 99 / Siskiyou Blvd. Turn right onto Siskiyou Blvd. and proceed one mile to where the road veers right onto Lithia Way. Continue to N 1st Street and turn left / south. Proceed one block to the Ashland Springs Hotel.

Lodging Option: The Winchester Inn

Originally a single farm style home built in 1887, today the quaint Winchester Inn consists of five buildings, each offering 5-star hotel amenities. Guests can choose from 21 luxurious rooms, each with down feather beds, 600 thread count sheets, down pillows and comforters, and a serving of pastry treats delivered each afternoon. Being a B & B, each morning includes a complimentary two-course breakfast.

    The Winchester Inn
    35 South 2nd Street
    Ashland, OR 97520
    541-488-1113

Driving Directions: The Winchester Inn is located one block east of the Ashland Springs Hotel on South 2nd Street.

SEE A PLAY IN ASHLAND

Each year, Ashland is host to the Oregon Shakespeare Festival. Running from mid-February to early November, the festival features eleven different plays performed on stage in three theatres near Lithia Park; the Angus Bowmer Theatre, Thomas Theatre and the impressive 1,200 seat Allen Elizabethan Theatre. Playgoers can choose between performances featuring the classic works of Shakespeare or more contemporary tales, all showcasing a wealth of acting talent.

There are 750 to 800 performances during each 10-month festival season, so inquire about seeing a play during your stay in Ashland. Visit www.OSFAshland.org to learn more.

www.Discover-Oregon.com

Notes

Day Three

Ashland to Jacksonville

Day 3
Ashland to Jacksonville

Day 3 – Date: /   /

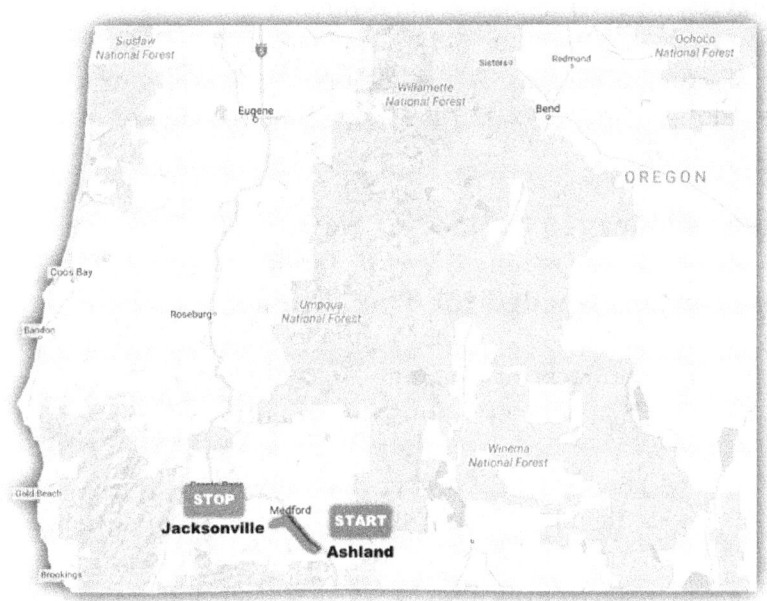

Summary: Where You're Going Today

- Ashland, OR
- Talent, OR
- Medford, OR
- Central Point, OR
- Jacksonville, OR

Today, you'll travel a short distance, only 26 miles, into the "heart" of Southwest Oregon, where you'll blend a sense of Oregon history with a taste of some of its finest wines, fruits and confections. Take your time to explore and enjoy today.

Tonight's Lodging:

- Historic Jacksonville Inn - **2 Nights**

Before You Leave:

Today's journey finishes in Jacksonville, OR. There are no gas stations in "old town" Jacksonville, so you'll want to fuel up before arriving. Look to get gas along the way, perhaps in Talent, OR or Medford, OR.

Today's Mileage: 26 Miles

Reservations Needed for This Segment:

- Historic Jacksonville Inn - 541-899-1900
    - Make reservations for **2 nights**

- The Jacksonville Trolley - 541-899-8118
    - Decide if you'd like to take this trolley tour later today, or early tomorrow morning. The last departure time today is at 2:30 p.m., and the first trolley tomorrow is at 10:30 a.m. See Page 78 for additional details. Reservations are not required.

- Harry & David Tour - 877-322-8000
    - Reservations are not required, but are highly recommended, especially during the fall.

Start

Today begins with breakfast and a casual stroll through a beautiful Ashland park and street market before driving west a relatively short distance to historic Jacksonville, OR, where a stay at the historic Jacksonville Inn awaits.

☐ **First Stop**: Breakfast at the Morning Glory Cafe

Offering breakfast, lunch and libations, the very popular Morning Glory Café is known throughout Southwest Oregon for its generous portions of good food made with fresh local ingredients. You may need to wait to get in.

Morning Glory Café
1149 Siskiyou Blvd.
Ashland, OR 97520
541-488-8638

- Open 8:00 a.m. – 1:30 p.m. – 7 Days a week

Driving Directions: From the Ashland Springs Hotel, proceed east on Siskiyou Blvd. for approximately one mile to the restaurant on your left. Parking is available in back, as well as at the motel next door, which may be more convenient, as the lot behind the restaurant is somewhat tight.

☐ **Ashland Stop**: Lithia Park

Start today with a pleasant stroll through Lithia Park, which is much larger than its first impression, as it stretches a considerable distance to the south. Enjoy its shady paths as they meander along babbling Ashland Creek, and then be sure to make your way to the northern end of the park to peruse the handmade wares of the Lithia Artisans Market.

Directions: From the Ashland Springs Hotel, *walk* south on S 1st Street to Hargadine Street. Turn right here and proceed a long block to a park entrance at S. Pioneer Street.

☐ **Ashland Stop**: Lithia Artisans Market

Located just off Winburn Way is the Lithia Artisans Market, a collection of booths offering high quality locally crafted items, including jewelry, clothing, art work, photography, fine prints, pottery, and more. Shop, visit with the artists and listen to live music. Continue north through the market to E Main Street, where you'll find additional shops.

- Open on weekends - Saturdays 10:00 a.m. - 6:00 p.m. and Sundays 11:00 a.m. - 5:00 p.m.

Directions: After wandering through Lithia Park, make your way to the western edge of the park, where you'll find Winburn Way. Follow this north to the Lithia Artisans Market on Calle Guanajuato, which is a small alleyway next to a park.

☐ **Next Stop**: Talent Historical Society Museum

Stop in and learn about the history of Talent, Oregon.

    Talent Historical Society Museum
    105 North Market Street
    Talent, OR 97540

- Open Saturdays and Sundays, 1:00 p.m. to 5:00 p.m.

Driving Directions: From the Ashland Springs Hotel, drive north one block to Lithia Way and turn left / northwest. Proceed on Lithia Way as it merges with N Main Street, eventually becoming Hwy 99 / South Pacific Highway. At approximately 5 miles from the Ashland Springs Hotel, turn left / south at a large intersection onto W Valley View Road and turn right / enter onto E Main Street at the roundabout. Continue on E Main Street to S Market Street and turn right / west. The Talent Historical Museum will be on your left.

☐ **Medford, OR Stop:** Harry & David Tour

Famous throughout Oregon, the Northwest and around the world, Harry & David fruits, candies and confections are made right here, in Medford, Oregon. Take a one hour tour to see how they craft their delicious chocolates and truffles, pop and prepare their popular Moose Munch® popcorn, process their world-famous Royal Riviera® pears, and package it all for shipment around the world. Tours of their 55-acre campus are given four times a day, Monday through Friday. Reservations are not required, but are highly recommended, especially during August and October when they are busy working to meet the demand of the coming Christmas season.

Note: Tours are $5 per person and begin at the Harry & David Country Village. Children ages 12 and under are free.

Harry & David Country Village
1314 Center Drive
Medford, OR
541-864-2278

- Reservations: 877-322-8000 or 541-864-2278
- Tours are given at 9:15 a.m., 10:30 a.m., 12:30 p.m. and 1:45 p.m.
- Please arrive 5 to 10 minutes early to check in

Driving Directions: From the Talent Historical Society Museum, return to Hwy 99. Turn left / northwest and proceed for approximately 6 miles to E Stewart Ave. Turn right / north here and proceed one block to Center Drive. Turn right / east onto Center Drive and proceed one block to Armory Drive. Turn right / south onto Armory Drive and then immediately turn into the parking lot to your right. Harry & David Country Village is to your left.

Note: There is ample parking in the parking lot here. RV parking is also available in the Fred Meyer parking lot directly across the street

☐ Medford, OR Stop: Medford Railroad Park

Medford's Railroad Park is a 49 acre parcel home to a collection of full-sized rolling stock, including a caboose, hopper car and locomotive, as well as a miniature steam train, which offers rides to visitors from 11:00 a.m. to 3:00 p.m. on the 2nd and 4th Sunday of each month from April through October. Rides are free, but donations are gladly accepted.

    Medford Railroad Park
    799 Berrydale Ave.
    Medford, OR 97501
    541-774-2400

Driving Directions: From Harry & David, return to Hwy 99 / S Pacific Hwy and turn right / northwest. Now on Hwy 99, proceed for 2.7 miles to W Table Rock Road, found shortly after passing the Rogue Valley Mall. Turn right / north onto W Table Rock Road and in 0.2 miles turn right / northwest onto Berrydale Ave.

☐ **Central Point, OR Stop:** Lillie Belle Farms Handmade Chocolates

Southwest Oregon is home to some of the world's finest award-winning wines, cheeses, orchard fruits and more. Of course, what goes with all of these? Chocolate! Stop in at Lillie Belle Farms Handmade Chocolates to explore and enjoy a mix of locally made artisan truffles, bon-bons, caramels and, of course, gourmet chocolates.

> Lillie Belle Farms Handmade Chocolates
> 211 N. Front Street
> Central Point, OR 97502
> 541-664-2815

- Open Monday through Friday – 9:00a.m. – 5:00 p.m.
- Saturdays – 9:00 a.m. – 6:00 p.m.
- Sundays – 11:00 a.m. – 5:00 p.m.

Note: Don't forget...you can order these chocolates by mail order for any special occasion any time you'd like once you're back home.

Driving Directions: From the Medford Railroad Park, return to Hwy 99. Turn right / northwest onto Hwy 99 and follow this 2¾ miles, as it becomes S Front Street, to Lillie Belle Farms Handmade Chocolates on your left.

☐ **Central Point, OR Stop:** Rogue Creamery Cheese Shop

Visit the Rogue Creamery Cheese Shop in Central Point, OR to learn how this historic creamery makes its cheese, as well as have a rare opportunity to experience "the best blue cheese in the world." In addition, you can try an abundance of cheese samples, enjoy a tasty grilled cheese sandwich, savor an assortment of Rogue Ales, root beers and local wines, and sample fine specialty foods from Southern Oregon.

Rogue Creamery (Hwy 99 / N. Pacific Hwy)
311 North Front Street
Central Point, OR 97502
541-665-1155

- Open
  - Monday through Friday 9:00 a.m. – 5:00 p.m.
  - Saturday 9:00 a.m. – 6:00 p.m.
  - Sunday 11:00 a.m. – 5:00 p.m.

Driving Directions: The Rogue Creamery Cheese Shop is right next door to Lillie Belle Farms Handmade Chocolates.

☐ Central Point, OR Stop: Crater Rock Museum

Established in 1952, this is one of the finest collections of rocks, minerals, gems, "thunder eggs" and fossils found on the West Coast.

Crater Rock Museum
2002 Scenic Ave.
Central Point, OR 97502
541-664-6081

- Open Tuesday through Saturday – 10:00 a.m. – 4:00 p.m.
- Adults $7 - Students $4 - Seniors & Veterans $5

Driving Directions: From the Rogue Creamery Cheese Shop, proceed west/northwest on Hwy 99 for a little over 1 mile to Scenic Ave. Turn right / east onto Scenic Ave. and proceed a short distance to the Crater Rock Museum.

www.Discover-Oregon.com

Tonight's Lodging- Historic Jacksonville Inn Jacksonville, OR

Tonight, you'll be staying at the beautiful Jacksonville Inn Bed and Breakfast in downtown Jacksonville, OR. Built in 1861, this award-winning historic inn welcomes guests with a selection of eight renovated hotel rooms and four small off-site cottages, as well as fine dining and an impressive reception area, which doubles as a wine cellar and store.

Jacksonville Inn Cottage Interior

> Jacksonville Inn
> 175 E California St.
> Jacksonville, OR 97530
> 541-899-1900

Note: You will be making reservations here for **2 nights**, or consider staying one night here and one night at The 1916 TouVelle House B & B or The Magnolia Inn. (Following pages)

Driving Directions: At 2 blocks east of Lillie Belle Farm Handmade Chocolates on Hwy 99, turn south onto W Pine Street and follow this for 5.3 miles as it turns into Hanley Road and then Hwy 238 to Jacksonville, OR. Upon reaching Jacksonville, turn right / west to find the Jacksonville Inn on your right in one block. Parking is available in a lot behind the inn, off N 4th Street.

Lodging Option #1: The 1916 TouVelle House B&B

Note: You will be making reservations for **2 nights**.

Located only two blocks from the heart of old town Jacksonville is the historic TouVelle House Bed & Breakfast. This 1916 Craftsman style home sits on over an acre of beautifully landscaped grounds and offers six elegantly appointed rooms with modern comforts, each with their own private bathroom. A three course breakfast is included with your stay, and for those who want a refreshing dip on a hot summer day, the TouVelle House offers its own pool for guests' use.

TouVelle House
455 N Oregon St.
Jacksonville, OR 97530
541-899-8938

The TouVelle House does have a two-night minimum *over the weekends* from Memorial Day weekend through the end of September, though one night stays sometimes become available. Inquire when making your reservations.

Note: The TouVelle House is unable to accommodate children under 12, as well as pets.

Driving Directions: Upon reaching Jacksonville, drive west on E California Street, the main street through town, and turn right / north onto N Oregon Street. Continue 4 blocks to find the TouVelle House on your left.

Lodging Option #2: Jacksonville's Magnolia Inn

Note: You will be making reservations for **2 nights**.

Located in the heart of Jacksonville, the stately and award-winning Jacksonville's Magnolia Inn welcomes guests with nine well-appointed historic rooms, each with a private bath, modern amenities and comfortable accommodations. Guests will enjoy a delicious continental breakfast featuring locally sourced fresh baked goods, fruits, and juices before exploring any of the many shops, restaurants and historic attractions nearby.

Jacksonville's Magnolia Inn
245 North 5th Street
Jacksonville, OR 97530
541-899-0255

- Check-in is between 3:00 p.m. and 8:00 p.m. everyday.

Note: Jacksonville's Magnolia Inn is a pet-friendly inn, with one room dedicated to pet owners.

Driving Directions: Jacksonville's Magnolia Inn is located on N 5th Street, two blocks north of E California Street, the main street through town.

Notes

Day Four

Explore Jacksonville, OR

DAY 4
EXPLORE JACKSONVILLE, OR

Day 4 – Date: /   /

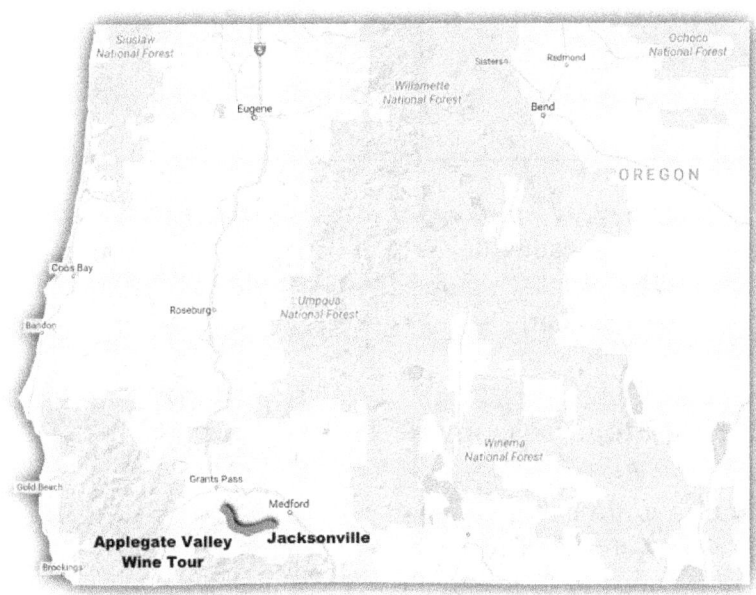

Summary: Where You're Going Today

- Explore Jacksonville, OR
- Tour the Applegate Valley Wine Trail

You'll begin today casually exploring the shops, buildings and interesting history of Jacksonville before driving out west on Hwy 238 to tour the award-winning vineyards and wineries of the Applegate Valley Wine Trail. If you so choose, you can finish your day dining at the DANCIN Vineyards, voted the 2017 Oregon Winery of the Year!

Tonight's Lodging:

- You'll stay a second night at the Jacksonville Inn

Today's Mileage: 80 to 120 Miles

Reservations Needed for This Segment:

- The Jacksonville Trolley – 541-899-8118
- Segway Tours of Jacksonville: 541-899-5269

Start

Begin your day by enjoying a casual breakfast before walking over to the Jacksonville Trolley stop / Jacksonville Visitor Center at 185 North Oregon Street in time for the first tour of the day at 10:30 a.m.

☐ **First Stop:** Jacksonville Trolley Tour

In addition to being a small and friendly town in the heart of wine country, Jacksonville, OR is rich in history and architecture. We highly recommend beginning your exploration of the area with the 45 minute Jacksonville Trolley Tour so as to get a sense of the town, its layout of attractions, and its history, all conveyed with a friendly and informative narrated trolley ride. The first trolley of the day runs at 10:30 a.m.

> Jacksonville Trolley Tours
> 185 North Oregon
> Jacksonville, OR 97530
> 541-899-8118

- Runs daily from June through September, and Fridays, Saturdays, Sundays & Mondays, May through October.

- Departs from the Visitor Info Center at the corner of C Street and North Oregon, next to the Post Office.

- Five tours a day, departing at 10:30 a.m., 11:30 a.m., 12:30 p.m., 1:30 p.m., and 2:30 p.m.

- Fare: Adults: $6.00 – Children: $3.00

- Tickets may be purchased at the Visitor Information Center. Reservations are not required.

- Note: As an option, if you have time in your schedule when you arrive in Jacksonville on Day 3, (yesterday) you can take the 2:30 p.m. tour.

Driving / Walking Directions: From the Jacksonville Inn, drive or walk west for 2 blocks on E California Street to N Oregon Street. Turn right / north and proceed 1 block to the Jacksonville Visitor Center and trolley stop on your left.

☐ Jacksonville Stop: Segway of Jacksonville

The future meets the past. Well, it rolls right by, actually. Take a two hour tour of Jacksonville's history via a Segway personal transporter. You'll spend 30 minutes becoming familiar with using a Segway before departing with your group on a two-hour tour through Nunan Square with its Victorian-style homes, past the historic courthouse and jail, and then up to the beautiful Britt Gardens before finishing at the historic Jacksonville Cemetery. Each tour is focused on the guest experience, and your guide is happy to customize it to the group's interests.

Segway of Jacksonville
360 N. Oregon Street
Jacksonville, OR 97530
541-899-5269
Info@SegwayofJacksonville.com

Hours:

Summer:

- June through September – Operates Mondays through Saturdays - 9:30 a.m. to 5:00 p.m. The primary tour departure times are at 10:00 a.m. and 2:00 p.m., though other times may be available, so contact Segway of Jacksonville for additional information.

- Sundays - 12:30 p.m. to 5:00 p.m. Note that tours on Sundays and Mondays require a reservation.

- Evening tours are also available, and these begin at approximately 5:00 p.m., depending upon if it is early or late summer.

- One hour "Glide and Dine" lunch or dinner tours are also available. Inquire for more information.

Winter:

- October through May – Operates Tuesdays through Saturdays – 10:00 a.m. to 4:00 p.m., or by appointment.

Note:

- Cost is $75 per person
- Reservations are suggested, but walk-ins are welcome
- Riders must be 14 years of age or older
- Riders must weigh 100 lbs or more
- Tours occur rain or shine, so dress accordingly.

Driving / Walking Directions: From the Jacksonville Inn, drive or walk west for 2 blocks on E California Street to N Oregon Street. Turn right / north and proceed a little less than 3 blocks to find Segway of Jacksonville on your right.

☐ Jacksonville Stop: The Beekman Bank

In 1857, Cornelius Beekman began operation of what would become Beekman Bank, a local institution in the heart of downtown Jacksonville, one which processed a reported $10 million in gold mined from the surrounding area. Mr. Beekman died in 1915, and before doing so, he directed that his bank should be preserved intact as a museum after his death. His wish was carried out through the years, and today visitors can step inside its doors and over 100 years back in time to see how the bank existed when Mr. Beekman worked there, complete with the original furnishings, notes, records, gold scales, and more.

> Beekman Bank Museum
> 110 W Californian Street
> Jacksonville, OR 97530
> 541-245-3650
> 541-773-6536
> Info@HistoricJacksonville.org

Note: Doors to access only the foyer area and its exhibits open at 10:00 a.m. Self-guided tours inside the Beekman Bank itself are also offered between 11:00 a.m. and 4:00 p.m. on Thursdays through Mondays, from Memorial Day weekend through Labor Day. Typically, a visit lasts about 30 minutes, and a docent is on hand to explain the history of Cornelius Beekman and his bank, the oldest in the northwest. Admission is free, but a $2 donation is greatly appreciated.

Driving / Walking Directions: The Beekman Bank is located 1 block west of the Jacksonville Inn, on the southeast corner of E California Street and N 3rd Street.

☐ Jacksonville Stop: The Beekman House

Tour the 1870s Gothic Revival home of Cornelius Beekman, owner of the Beekman Bank and one-time Mayor of Jacksonville. As with the Beekman Bank, the home is preserved and presented just as it appeared in 1911.

Two tours of the home are offered:

- **Victorian Theme Tours** – Offers a look at the daily life of the Beekmans as they lived in Jacksonville during the late 1800s. Tours depart every 15 minutes from 11:00 a.m. to 3:00 p.m. on the 3rd Saturday of each month, May through September. $5.00 for Adults. No reservations are required. Tours are also offered on the 3rd Saturday *and* Sunday of October, though with a different theme.

- **1932 Living History Tours** – Enter the Beekman home and step back in time to 1932 to witness Ben and Carrie Beekman sorting through the home after their mother's passing. Interact with them as they reminisce and comment on life with their parents and happenings in Jacksonville clear back to the late 1800s.

Living History Tours occur at 12:00 noon, 1:00 p.m., and 3:00 p.m. on the 4th Saturday of each month, May through September. $8.00 for Adults, $5.00 for seniors and students. Each tour takes approximately one hour.

Note: Cash or check only. No credit cards are accepted.

The Beekman House
470 E California St.
Jacksonville, OR 97530
541-245-3650

Photo courtesy of the Jacksonville Review

Driving / Walking Directions: From the Beekman Bank, proceed east on E California Street for ¼ mile to the Beekman House on your right.

☐ **Jacksonville Stop:** Guided Cemetery Tour

Atop a hill in Jacksonville is one of Oregon's largest and oldest cemeteries, with its first burial dating back to over 150 years ago. Divided into seven sections for different faiths and organizations, ornate tombstones tell a story of the hardships endured by those who came to the Jacksonville area from all across the United States, as well as overseas, to seek a better life in Oregon many, many years ago.

Jacksonville Cemetery
Cemetery Road
Jacksonville, OR 97530
541-899-1231

The cemetery is open to the public seven days a week year-round for self-guided tours from 8:00 a.m. until ½ hour after dusk. Ninety minute guided interpretive tours of the cemetery are also offered to the public:

- Morning Tour: Second Saturday of each month, May through September – Meet at the cemetery at 10:00 a.m.

- Evening Tour: Second Tuesday of each month, May through August - Meet at the cemetery at 6:30 p.m.

Meet your Docents at the Sexton Tool House at the top of Cemetery Road. Parking is available within cemetery grounds.

No advance registration is required. The tours are free, but donations are greatly appreciated so as to help support the cemetery's educational programs, as well as the constant cemetery restoration and preservation work.

Driving / Walking Directions: From the Beekman House, return west on E California Street for a little over ¼ mile to N Oregon Street. Turn right / north here and proceed 3 blocks to Cemetery Road. Turn left and follow the road up the hill.

☐ Jacksonville Stop: The Nunan Estate

Located on three manicured acres on Oregon Street is the most photographed home in Jacksonville, the Nunan Estate. An impressive Queen Anne style home, it was built in 1892 by Jacksonville pioneer Jeremiah Nunan from plans created by George F. Barber, the same architect who designed the Goeller House, which you saw in Klamath Falls on Day 2 of your road trip. Inside this 4,000 square foot home one will find five bedrooms, two parlors, five fireplaces, a ballroom, an elaborate dining room and more. Note: This is a private home and is not open to the public, though the Onyx Restaurant & Bar next door is.

Holding up to 10 guests, the Nunan Estate may be rented for overnight stays. Learn more about the estate and its availability online.

The Nunan House
635 North Oregon Street
Jacksonville, OR 97530

The Onyx Restaurant & Bar

Next door to the Nunan Estate is the new "gastro-pub" style Onyx Restaurant, featuring an eclectic menu offering local fare and award-winning wines of Southern Oregon.

- Dinner: Tuesday through Saturday, 5:00 p.m. to 8:30 p.m.

- 541-702-2700

Driving / Walking Directions: From the Jacksonville Cemetery, return down the hill to N Oregon Street. Turn left and proceed north for ¼ mile to the Nunan Estate on your left.

www.Discover-Oregon.com

The Applegate Valley Wine Trail

Stretching west from Jacksonville is the scenic Applegate Valley, home of some of Oregon's finest wine country. Here, 17 different vineyards and wineries practice their craft to produce award-winning wines known around the world. Each of these wineries welcomes visitors via the Applegate Valley Wine Trail, a meandering route off of Hwy 238, which winds its way along country backroads visiting one winery after another. Make your way along the route and spend the day exploring different wineries, walking through vineyards, talking with the vintners, and sampling an amazing collection of wines, perhaps even while sitting in a chair next to a gently flowing creek. If your timing is right, you may even catch some live music or another special event. Spot a winery and drive on in!

Driving Directions: From Jacksonville, drive west out of town on E California Street, which becomes Hwy 238. Follow this 7 miles to the town of Ruch, OR, the beginning of the Applegate Valley Wine Tour. See the map on the next page as your guide.

www.Discover-Oregon.com

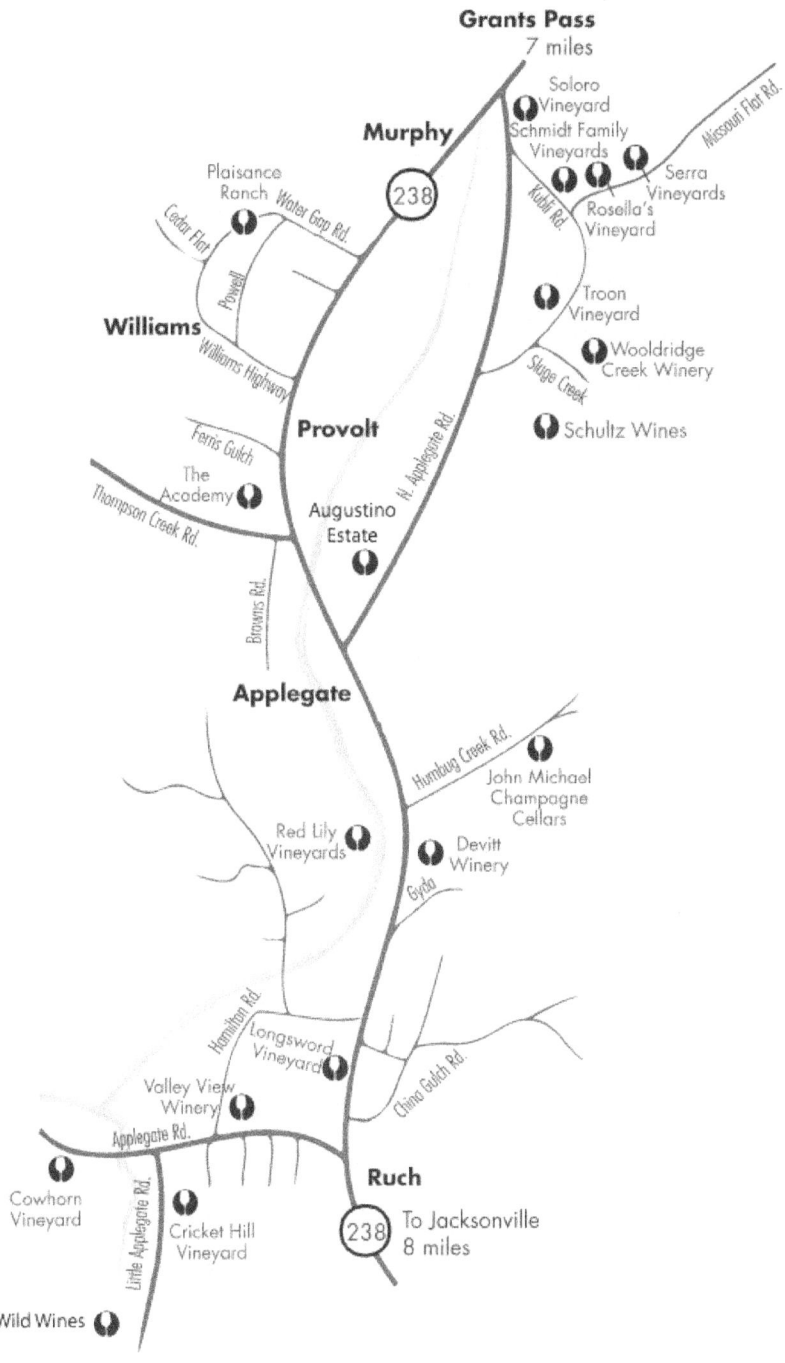

☐ **Applegate Valley Wine Trail Stop:** McKee Covered Bridge

Your next stop is at the McKee Covered Bridge. Built in 1917 to carry miners and loggers across the Applegate River, this picturesque bridge features unique flying buttresses on each side, the first covered bridge on this road trip to do so.

Directions: From Jacksonville, head west on Hwy 238 into the Applegate Valley to Ruch, OR. At approximately 8 miles from Jacksonville, turn south from Hwy 238 onto Upper Applegate Road and continue for approximately 8.5 miles to McKee Bridge Road. Turn left / south here and follow this dead end road 500 feet to the covered bridge.

Bridge photo courtesy of www.MedfordMom.com

☐ **Applegate Valley Wine Trail Stop:** Applegate Valley Lavender Farm

If it's July, then all of the lavender plants at the Applegate Valley Lavender Farm are in bloom, and it's quite a sight to see, as row upon row of purple blossoms fill the field. Being a farm, you'll also find a collection of Olde English Babydoll Sheep, Sebastopol Geese, ducks, chickens, roosters and more.

Applegate Valley Lavender Farm
15370 Hwy 238
Grants Pass, OR 97527
541-291-9229

Open: Thursday through Sunday - 10:00 a.m. to 4:00 p.m. Call for details about their Golden Hour Harvest evening hours, which typically run from 6:00 p.m. to 8:00 p.m. Times can vary, however, due to the bloom, weather and local conditions.

Driving Directions: You'll find the Applegate Valley Lavender Farm 1 mile east of the town of Provolt, OR, just off Hwy 238.

☐ **Applegate Valley Wine Trail Stop:** The Great Unbaked Chocolate Factory

What goes well with award-winning Oregon wines? Award-winning chocolate, of course! Be sure to stop in at the Great Unbaked Chocolate Factory during your winery tour to sample *"the best vegan, raw, organic chocolates handcrafted in southern Oregon."* You'll find truffle bars, truffle balls, fudge brownies, chocolate frosting and even raw dark chocolate chips, which are guaranteed to give you a bit of a kick. It's all hand-crafted in this small shop, so pop in and say hello. Note the fun school next door, too.

The Great Unbaked Chocolate Factory
8880 Williams Hwy - Unit B
Grants Pass, OR 97527
541-450-9080

- Open Monday through Thursday - 9:30 a.m. to 4:00 p.m., Friday - 10:30 a.m. to 3:00 p.m.

Driving Directions: You'll find The Great Unbaked Chocolate Factory approximately 2.5 miles east of Murphy, OR, just off Hwy 238, at the west end of the Applegate Valley Wine Trail. Note: Google Maps may send you ¼ mile too far west.

☐ Jacksonville Stop: DANCIN Vineyards

Finish your day at one of the area's finest award-winning vineyards, and stay for a while to sample fine wines, wood-fired pizza, and delicious fare, all with beautiful Southern Oregon views.

DANCIN Winery
4477 South Stage Rd.
Medford, OR 97501
541-245-1133

- Open:

  - May through September - Thursday through Sunday - 12:00 p.m. - 8:00 p.m., Wednesday - 4:00 p.m. to 8:00 p.m.

  - October through April - Thursday through Sunday - 12:00 p.m. - 7:00 p.m.

Driving Directions: From the Jacksonville Inn, proceed approximately 1.3 miles east on E California Street / S Stage Rd., where you'll find the entrance to DANCIN on your right.

☐ Last Stop: The Jacksonville Inn

Stay your second night in Jacksonville at the Jacksonville Inn.

Notes

www.Discover-Oregon.com

Day Five

Jacksonville to Idleyld Park - Roseburg

Day 5
Jacksonville to
Idleyld Park - Roseburg

Day 5 – Date: /   /

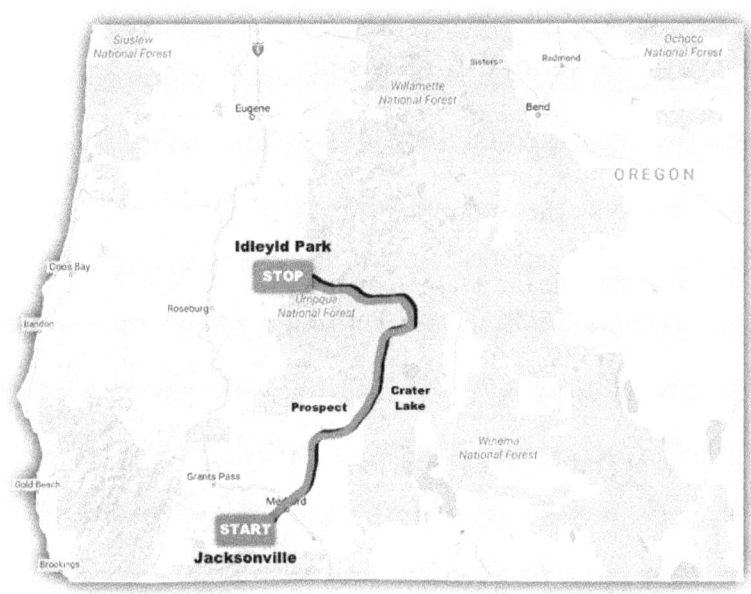

Summary: Where You're Going Today

- Jacksonville, OR
- Trail, OR
- Prospect, OR
- Union Creek, OR
- Rogue Gorge
- Diamond Lake, OR
- Idleyld Park, OR

Today takes you along the Rogue-Umpqua Scenic Byway, where you'll enjoy driving through the beautiful Umpqua National Forest, taking in stops to see churning whitewater, a towering waterfall, and dramatic views of 9,183' Mt. Thielsen before turning west along the Umpqua River towards your destination for the evening, the tranquil Steamboat Inn.

Tonight's Lodging:

- The Steamboat Inn

Today's Mileage: 130 Miles

Reservations Needed for This Segment:

- The Steamboat Inn - 541-498-2230

- Dinner at the Steamboat Inn - Dinner is optional, but if you chose to eat at the hotel, you must make reservations at least two days in advance. Dinner is served at 5:30 p.m. Let them know of any dietary restrictions you may have when you make your dinner reservations.

- The Wood House - Interior Reservations - 541-826-2177

Start

Travel north out of Jacksonville through Medford and Eagle Point, where you'll join the Crater Lake Highway / Rogue-Umpqua Scenic Byway and follow this northwest to Diamond Lake, before turning back west towards Idleyld Park and the nearby Steamboat Inn.

Before You Leave:

Fill your gas tank in Medford, just beyond your first stop of the day.

☐ Central Point, OR Stop: Hanley Farm

Stop in and visit the historic Hanley Farm, an 1857 farmstead operated by the Southern Oregon Historical Society. In addition to seeing a working farm, you'll learn about the people who settled and farmed the lands of the Rogue Valley and their important contributions to the agricultural development of the area. In addition, the Hanley Farm often holds interpretive and entertaining events, such as the Living History Days and frequent live music performances. Tours are self-guided, so feel free to park and walk around the farm. You'll find tour brochures at the Greeting Board by the water tower.

Hanley Farm
1053 Hanley Rd.
Central Point, OR 97502
541-773-6536

Driving Directions: From the Jacksonville Inn, drive east on E California Street for 1 block and turn left / north onto N 5th Street / Hwy 238. Continue north for 2.4 miles to the farm on your left.

☐ Eagle Point, OR Stop: The Wood House

Your second stop of the day takes you all the way back to 1870 with a visit to The Wood House. Built by Civil War Veteran Marvin Sylvester Wood, this home has an amazing history, one which saw its near demise on numerous occasions, only to be saved by concerned Oregonians each time to become a treasured piece of Oregon history and the most photographed home in the northwest. Today, it welcomes visitors at anytime to stop and see just how Oregonians lived in the late 1800s.

> The Wood House
> 12988 Hwy 62
> Eagle Point, OR 97524
> 541-826-2177

Note: The Wood House does not have any set hours. You can view the home from the fence on the parkway out front, or you may tour the home if volunteers are there when you visit. In addition, you may call 541-826-2177 to make an appointment to see inside the home, and this should be done one week in advance of your arrival.

Driving Directions: From the Hanley Farm, continue north on Hwy 238 for a little under ½ mile to a stop. Turn right / east here and continue on Hwy 238 through Medford as it becomes Hwy 62 / Crater Lake Hwy. At approximately 15 miles, just north of Eagle Point, you'll find the Wood House to your right, immediately off Hwy 62.

Photo courtesy of The Wood House Preservation Group

☐ **Next Stop:** Trail Creek Tavern Museum

Off the beaten path in Trail, OR is the Upper Rogue Historical Society's Trail Creek Tavern Museum. Located in a former tavern, this intriguing museum and its surrounding three acres showcases life in the Upper Rogue area during the early years of its settlement, as well as the timber, ranching and sport fishing industries that were so important to the economy here.

Trail Creek Tavern Museum
144 Old Highway 62
Trail, OR 97541
541-621-4462

- Open Thursday through Sunday, mid-April to October 1 – 10:00 a.m. to 4:00 p.m.

Note: If the museum isn't open when you stop by, the docent lives onsite, so feel free to call the number above, and he'll walk over and open the museum for you. Note that he will not turn on the heat during the winter, however.

Driving Directions: From the Wood House, travel north on the Crater Lake Hwy for approximately 10.5 miles to Old Trail Creek Road. Turn left / west here and proceed 0.2 miles to the Trail Creek Tavern Museum on your right. Note: There is gas available a few miles north of Trail.

☐ **Next Stop:** Mill Creek Falls & Barr Creek Falls

An easy trail leads you to two of the highest waterfalls on the Rogue River, Mill Creek Falls and Barr Creek Falls. Find the parking lot on the right with the large wooden map reading "Mill Creek Falls Scenic Area". From the trailhead, as indicated on the map, hike to the junction for Avenue of the Boulders (left) and Mill Creek Falls and Barr Creek Falls (right). Continue right from the junction for a short distance to find Mill Creek Falls plunging 173' to the river below on the opposite side of the canyon. Continue following the trail for less than ¼ mile to find Barr Creek Falls tumbling as a cascade before falling as a ribbon below.

Note: Avenue of the Boulders, to the left, is an interesting site, but can be dangerous for young children and pets, given the slippery boulders and their proximity to the fast moving river, especially in the spring.

Driving Directions: From the Trail Creek Tavern Museum, return to the Crater Lake Highway and proceed left / north for 15.3 miles to the paved Mill Creek Drive, just past Mile Post 42. Turn right / east here and continue for a little over 5 miles, following the signs to the large parking area and trailhead on the right.

☐ **Next Stop:** Mill Creek Bridge and the Avenue of Giant Boulders

Stop and enjoy the 1930s era architecture of the beautiful Mill Creek Bridge before taking a short path to overlook a dramatic tumbling cascade above the Avenue of Giant Boulders. Be mindful of little ones, as the short trail leads to a high cliff without a railing above the water.

You'll find the short trail begins on the other side of the guardrail on the south side of the bridge.

Driving Directions: From the Mill Creek Falls and Barr Creek Falls parking area, continue north on the Crater Lake Highway for less than ½ mile to the Mill Creek Bridge. Park in the small parking area on the north side of the bridge.

☐ **Next Stop:** Historic Prospect Hotel

A former stagecoach stop built in the late 1880s, the Historic Prospect Hotel welcomes guests with 10 period-specific rooms, each featuring antiques, a handmade bed quilt and floral print wallpaper. In addition, 14 modern motel units catering to large groups and those needing extra accessibility can be found behind the motel. Pets are allowed, but in the motel units only.

Prospect Historic Hotel
391 Mill Creek Drive
Prospect, OR 97536
541-560-3664

Note: Want to add an extra day to your trip and enjoy some additional time to explore the hikes and sights of this area? Both the Historic Prospect Hotel and the Union Creek Resort, just up the road, would make perfect destinations for the day. Stay overnight, and then continue on your way to Steamboat Inn tomorrow at a more leisurely pace. Just remember to make your reservations accordingly.

Driving Directions: The Prospect Historic Hotel is only a short distance north of the Mill Creek bridge.

☐ **Next Stop:** Natural Bridge Hike

This easy 2.4 mile loop trail takes you to a natural stone "land bridge" spanning the Rogue River. Watch the Rogue disappear into an ancient lava cave tube only to reappear a couple hundred feet downstream. The trail offers numerous viewpoints, along with interpretive signs which explain this geologic wonder. Note that if the river is running high, it will flow over the land bridge, covering it entirely.

Driving Directions: From the Prospect Historic Hotel, drive north for 0.6 miles to the Crater Lake Highway. Turn right / north and continue for 9.6 miles to the turnoff for the Natural Bridge Recreation Area. Turn left / west here and continue 0.2 miles to the trailhead for the Natural Bridge Hike.

☐ **Next Stop:** Union Creek, OR / Union Creek Resort

Spanning both sides of the Crater Lake Highway / Rogue-Umpqua Scenic Byway is the Union Creek Resort. Built in 1922, it consists of the Union Creek Lodge, its 9 rooms and 23 rustic yet modern cabins, a Country Store, Beckie's Café, Beckie's Chuckwagon, and an ice cream shop, all under the shade of towering Douglas Firs.

This may be about time for lunch, and here you have your choice between Beckie's Café and Beckie's Chuckwagon. The cafe offers inside table dining featuring homestyle cooking and fresh made pies, all in a welcoming rustic lodge setting, while the latter is an original version of the food cart, offering BBQ fare with the choices of beef, chicken and pulled pork.

Driving Directions: From the Natural Bridge hike parking lot, return to the Crater Lake Highway. Turn left / north and continue 1 mile to Union Creek, OR.

www.Discover-Oregon.com

☐ **Next Stop:** Rogue River Gorge Viewpoint

Located only a short distance off the Rogue-Umpqua Scenic Byway is the Rogue River Gorge, a long narrow chasm in the forest through which the Rogue River churns and falls as it makes its way downstream. Alongside, a short quarter mile interpretive trail offers numerous viewpoints of this interesting geologic feature.

Driving Directions: Proceed to the northern end of Union Creek and turn left onto the road which leads to the Rogue Gorge Viewpoint. The large parking lot here has restrooms.

☐ **Last Stop:** Toketee Falls

You finish today's journey with a visit to beautiful Toketee Falls. Flanked by moss covered basalt columns, this elegant waterfall plunges in two stages; a 28' drop into a churning whitewater pool carved into the basalt over the ages, followed by an 85' drop to a much larger pool below.

The ½ mile trail to a large viewing platform opposite the falls is rated "more difficult" due to its number of stairs, including 97 up and 125 down on the way there. Of course, it's just the opposite on the way back. If you arrive close to sunset on a summer day, you can view the falls with sunlight on them, which makes for beautiful photographs.

You'll notice in the parking area a large 12' diameter wooden pipe, which spouts numerous water leaks. Built in 1949, it diverts water from the North Umpqua River to a powerhouse below. If a leak is spraying near the roadway, it makes for an excellent opportunity to clean a buggy windshield. Just park underneath the spray and turn on your windshield wipers!

Driving Directions: Reset your odometer. From the Rogue River Gorge Viewpoint, proceed north on the Crater Lake Highway approximately 1¼ miles and merge left onto Highway 230 / W Diamond Lake Highway and continue to the 25 mile point, where you'll connect with Hwy 138. Turn left / north here onto Hwy 138 and follow this to Toketee-Rigdon Rd. / NF-34, 49 miles from where you started at the Rogue River Gorge Viewpoint. Turn right / north onto Toketee-Rigdon Rd. and follow this 0.2 miles to the turnoff for the Toketee Falls Trailhead, on your left.

www.Discover-Oregon.com

Tonight's Lodging - Steamboat Inn

After a full day of exploring Oregon on the Rogue-Umpqua Scenic Byway, you'll enjoy an evening relaxing at the quaint Steamboat Inn. Located beneath towering firs and deciduous maples on beautifully manicured grounds next to the majestic North Umpqua River, this historic Oregon lodge offers a welcome meal and nights rest to the adventurous road tripper.

Note: Arrive early enough and you will have time to take a short trail from the inn down to the river to sit for a while.

The Steamboat Inn offers Streamside Cabins, Hideaway Cottages, River Suites, and larger Camp Water Houses.

Note: You will be making reservations for **1 night**.

Steamboat Inn
42705 N Umpqua Hwy
Idleyld Park, OR 97447
541-498-2230
www.TheSteamboatInn.com

Driving Directions: From the Toketee Falls trailhead, return to Hwy 138 / Umpqua Scenic Byway and turn right / west. Proceed for 20.5 miles to the Steamboat Inn on your left.

Notes

Day Six

Idleyld Park – Roseburg to Grants Pass

Day 6
Idleyld Park – Roseburg to Grants Pass

Day 6 – Date: /   /

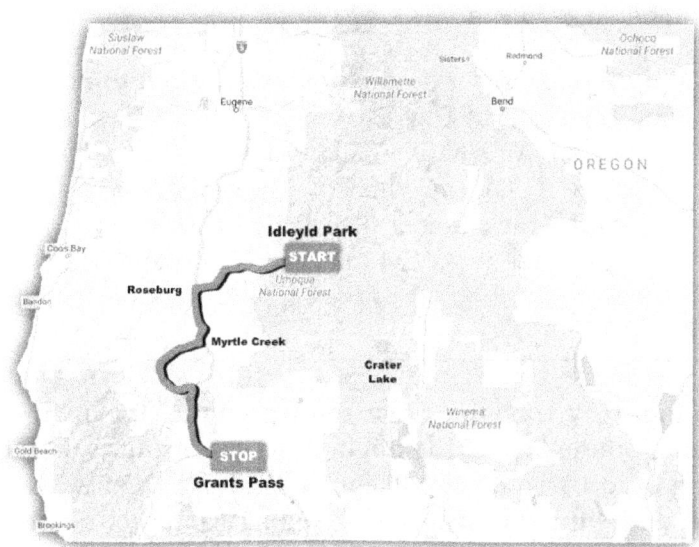

Summary: Where You're Going Today

- Glide, OR
- Roseburg, OR
- Myrtle Creek, OR
- Cow Creek Scenic Tour Route
- Wolf Creek, OR
- Golden, OR
- Grants Pass, OR

Today you'll travel deep into the beauty of Southwest Oregon, exploring the history of the area as you travel along the scenic Cow Creek Tour Route before turning towards the Wolf Creek Inn. From here, you'll continue south to Grants Pass and your destination for tonight, the Weasku Inn lodge.

Tonight's Lodging:

- The Weasku Inn

Today's Mileage: 170 Miles

Reservations Needed for This Segment:

- The Weasku Inn - 541-471-8000

- You'll make reservations for **two nights**; tonight (**Day 6**) and the night of **Day 8**
    - As an Alternative: Make a reservation for tonight, night 6, at the Weasku Inn and for night 8 at the Wolf Creek Inn or The Lodge at Riverside in Grants Pass. See Page 124 and 148 for details.

Start

Begin today by traveling west towards Glide, OR on Hwy 138, finishing up the last of the Rogue-Umpqua Scenic Byway before turning onto I-5 South in Roseburg, OR for a brief while before connecting with the scenic Cow Creek Tour Route. Heading west, you'll enjoy the scenery and history of this area as you travel along Cow Creek before reconnecting with I-5 South towards Grants Pass and your destination for tonight, the Weasku Inn lodge, just east of town.

☐ **First Stop**: Enjoy the North Umpqua River

Before you begin traveling today, take a moment to wander down to the river and enjoy the view in the early morning light.

☐ **Next Stop**: The Narrows on the North Umpqua River

18 Miles after leaving Steamboat Inn, you'll find two small pullouts on the left side of the road. Pull into either one and walk down a short fisherman's path to find "The Narrows" of the North Umpqua River.

☐ **Next Stop**: Colliding Rivers Viewpoint

At Colliding Rivers, you'll be treated to a sight which occurs nowhere else in the world. Here, the Little River meets the North Umpqua River head on, instead of merging from the side as all rivers do, creating an unusual roil of water and waves as these two powerful forces collide. Park in the parking area and look over the side to see all of the action.

Driving Directions: From Steamboat Inn, travel west on Hwy 138 / Umpqua Scenic Byway for 23.1 miles to the west end of Glide, OR and turn right / north onto Glide Loop Drive, where you'll see a parking area for the Colliding Rivers on your left.

www.Discover-Oregon.com

☐ Next Stop: Cavitt Creek Bridge – Glide, OR

Built in 1943, the Cavitt Creek Covered Bridge spans the serene Little River south of Glide, OR. It's interesting to note that the openings on each end of the bridge used to have a unique characteristic called a Tudor Portal Arch, in that they both rose to point, instead of a flat horizontal span, reaching nearly 19' high so as to allow fully loaded logging trucks to pass through with enough clearance.

Driving Directions: From the Colliding Rivers Viewpoint, return to Hwy 138 and turn right / west, followed almost immediately with a turn left / south onto Little River Road. Follow this for 6¾ miles south to Cavitt Creek Road. Turn right / south here and you'll see the Cavitt Creek covered bridge. Drive through and park on the far side.

☐ Next Stop: Douglas County Museum

Located just south of Roseburg is the Douglas County Museum, a large complex showcasing the history of Douglas County and Southwest Oregon. Here, you'll explore a large number of rooms, each with a wealth of interpretive displays showcasing the daily lives of the early pioneers, the natural and cultural history of the area, and the industries which have driven the economy for many decades. Outside, visitors will find antique farming equipment, a railroad depot, railroad rolling stock, antique autos and more. Be sure to find the fascinating display about the 1959 fire in downtown Roseburg, which ignited a truck parked on the street carrying a two ton load of dynamite and four and one-half tons of ammonium nitrate. The ensuing blast leveled eight city blocks and created a crater 52 feet wide and 12 feet deep.

Douglas County Museum
123 Museum Dr.
Roseburg, OR 97471
541-957-7007

- Open 10:00 a.m. – 5:00 p.m. – Tuesday through Saturday

Driving Directions: From the Cavitt Covered Bridge, return to Hwy 138 and turn left / west. Follow this 17 miles into Roseburg, OR, following the signs for I-5 South. Take I-5 South for approximately 1 mile to Exit 123. At the exit, turn left / east and, after passing under the freeway, turn right / south onto Frear Street. Follow this to the Douglas County Museum.

☐ **Next Stop**: Wildlife Safari – Winston, OR

Extend your Southern Oregon road trip to Africa, Asia and all of North America with a drive-through trek at Wildlife Safari. Featuring over 500 animals on 600 acres, you'll spot tigers, lions, elephants, hippos, rhinos, giraffes, bears, cheetahs, zebras, flamingos, bison, camels and much more. In addition, train rides are available, as well as a children's petting zoo, gift shop and restaurant, all on manicured grounds.

Note: You'll want to allow up to 1.5 hours to complete the drive-through portion of your visit.

Wildlife Safari
1790 Safari Road
Winston, OR 97496
541-679-6761
GuestServices@WildlifeSafari.net

- Adults: $21.95
- Children: $15.95
- Seniors: $18.95

- Hours of Operation:

    Mid-November – Mid-March

    > Drive-Thru: 10:00 a.m. – 4:00 p.m.
    > (Last vehicle admitted at 4:00 p.m.)
    > Closed Thanksgiving and Christmas

    Mid-March – Mid-November

    > Drive-Thru: 9:00 a.m. – 6:00 p.m.
    > (Last vehicle admitted at 5:00 p.m.)

Note: No pets are allowed in the Wildlife Safari Drive Though or the Safari Village. Kennels are available for pets for $5. Inquire at the gift shop.

Driving Directions: From the Douglas County Museum, return to I-5 and continue south to Exit 119. Take the exit and follow this as it merges onto Hwy 42 / N 99 heading southeast towards Winston. Continue 2¾ miles to Lookingglass Road. Turn right / west onto Lookingglass Road and follow this 0.2 miles to Safari Road. Turn right here and follow the signs to the Wildlife Safari.

www.Discover-Oregon.com

☐ **Next Stop**: Horse Creek Covered Bridge

Myrtle Creek, OR is home to two covered bridges; Horse Creek Covered Bridge and the Neal Lane Covered Bridge.

Located on the southern edge of Millsite Park in downtown Myrtle Creek, the 110' Horse Creek Bridge is closed to cars but provides pedestrian access to the park. Originally built in 1930 to span Horse Creek in Lane County, approximately 130 miles northwest of here, it was deconstructed in 1987 and its materials were moved to this site, where much of the bridge was rebuilt.

Driving Directions: From the Wildlife Safari, take I-5 south to Exit 108 and follow this a short distance to where it crosses a bridge and merges into N Main Street. Follow N Main Street and turn right / southeast onto 1st Ave. Park at Millsite Park. You'll find the Horse Creek bridge at the south end of the park.

☐ **Next Stop**: Neal Lane Covered Bridge

The second of Myrtle Creek's bridges, the Neal Lane Covered Bridge, is one of the shortest covered bridges in all of Oregon and can be found just south of town. Built in 1939 and spanning South Myrtle Creek, the bridge measures only 42' in length, just long enough to reach the other side of the creek!

Driving Directions: From 1ˢᵗ Ave. and S Main Ave. in Myrtle Creek, turn right / southeast onto S. Main Ave. and proceed for 2 blocks to East Riverside Dr. Turn left / east here and then turn right / south onto Days Creek Cutoff Road in 0.2 miles. Follow this for ¾ mile to SE Neal Lane, where you'll find the Neal Lane Covered Bridge.

☐ **Next Stop**: Little Suzie's Breakfast and Lunch Cafe

If you're getting a little hungry after checking the sights in Myrtle Creek, then Little Suzie's is the place to go.

Little Suzie's
920 N Old Pacific Hwy
Myrtle Creek, OR 97457
541-863-3963

Open: Monday through Friday – 7:00 a.m. to 3:00 p.m.

Driving Directions: From the Neal Lane Covered Bridge, return to the intersection with N. Main Street in Myrtle Creek. Turn left / southeast and proceed 1.6 miles to where you'll find Little Suzie's on your left, at the intersection with Weeks Road.

☐ **Next Stop**: Cow Creek Scenic Tour Route

For the next one to two hours, make your way along the Cow Creek Scenic Tour Route, a 45 mile drive through the canyons and valleys of Cow Creek. Along the way, you'll see many historical remnants, complete with interpretive signs, of the original Oregon & California Railroad route, which was built

1905 Photo of "Old Betsy"

in the 1870s and stretched from Portland to San Francisco, bringing economic opportunities to the entire Willamette Valley. In addition, this area was rich in gold mining activities, and today the mother lode consists of wildflowers in the spring, blazing leaf colors in the fall, and scenery all year-round.

Driving Directions: From Little Suzie's Cafe, head south on N. Old Pacific Hwy in front of the restaurant and follow this for 2.5 miles to where it curves west onto Gael Lane. Follow this over I-5 and stay on it as it becomes Riddle Bypass Road, bypassing Riddle, OR to the north. This road automatically becomes the Cow Creek Scenic Tour Route as it leaves Riddle.

Important: Reset your odometer as you pass the turn to Main Street northeast of Riddle, OR. (You do not turn onto Main Street) This will be your point of origin for the tour route.

☐ **Cow Creek Stop**: Fir Oak Farm Suspension Bridge

At approximately 12.5 miles from Riddle, OR, you'll see an interesting suspension bridge spanning Cow Creek. Unfortunately, this is closed to the public, as it is meant to provide private access to Fir Oak Farm, a small family farm across the creek growing certified organic top-quality fruits and vegetables.

www.Discover-Oregon.com

☐ Cow Creek Stop: Stone Wall & Bridges

At approximately 24.5 miles, you'll find a interpretive tribute in a pull out on your left to the multitude of Chinese craftsmen, stone masons, and laborers who not only helped build the railroad line along Cow Creek, but also much of the American west. Stop here to take note of the intricate stone work that makes up the wall on the opposite creek bed, as well as the interpretive signs which explain the history of the nearby area.

Important: At 23 miles, there is a 90 degree turn south, over a bridge, which is non-intuitive. It looks like you should continue going west, but turn here and go south over the bridge, as this is still Cow Creek Road. Look for the hand spray painted signs on the bridge curbs pointing drivers to Glendale.

☐ Cow Creek Stop: Tuller Family Grave Marker

At approximately 30.6 miles into the Cow Creek Scenic Tour Route, you'll find a pullout on the right side of the road overlooking a large clearcut vista. There, next to a large boulder, you'll find an interpretive sign which reads...

In this vicinity are buried Jeremiah G. Tuller, born in Ohio 1822, who came to Oregon in 1844, served in the Cayuse Indian war in 1847 and 1848. He died in 1895. His wife Miriam, born in Illinois in 1826, came to Oregon

in 1845 via the Barlow Road, and died in 1907. Their daughter, Clementine Bell M.D., born in 1852, graduated from the University of Oregon Medical School in 1899 and died in 1901. Another daughter, Edith Tuller, known locally as "the Hermit Lady", tended the family graves until her death in 1931. She is buried in the Glendale Cemetery. The Tuller home was destroyed by fire shortly after Edith's death.

Jeremiah and Miriam Tuller both made difficult journeys to Oregon via different paths. To learn more about the life of Miriam Tuller, her journey westward from Illinois, and how she met Jeremiah, see her account titled *Crossing the Plains in 1845*, which we have included on Page 155 of this book.

Finishing the Cow Creek Tour Route

To finish the Cow Creek Tour Route, continue driving south along the tour route to where Cow Creek Road becomes Reuben Road. (There is no signage. It just happens) Follow Reuben Road east into Glendale, OR and follow the signs to I-5. Turn right / south onto Azalea-Glen Road and then turn left / east onto Glendale Valley Road. Follow this for 2.4 miles to I-5.

☐ **Next Stop**: Wolf Creek Inn State Heritage Site

Back in the late 1800s, travelers throughout the northwest would make their way from town to town, inn to inn, and on a good day cover perhaps 25 miles by horse and buggy or by stage coach. Travelers in this part of Oregon would make their way along the Applegate Trail, and after a long day navigating poor roads and often wet weather, would welcome the comforts of the Wolf Creek Inn.

Built in 1883, the Wolf Creek Inn holds the distinction of being the oldest continuously operating inn in the Pacific Northwest. Today, it is operated by the Oregon State Parks & Recreation division, and its 8 well-furnished period-specific rooms welcome  travelers from not just the northwest, but from around the world, for only $80 per night. Stop by the inn for a self-guided tour, and be sure to ask about the ghost who resides in Room #8!

The Wolf Creek Tavern is open year-round, and reservations to stay here may be made via Reserve America at 800-452-5687. Kristy and I had a unique Oregon adventure when we stayed overnight at the Inn and were the only people in the entire building...save for the ghost!

Note: While the sign out front says the inn serves Tasty Cuisine, the restaurant is currently not in service. However, Ricki's Place right next door is not only very welcoming, but they serve excellent food, as well. (541-866-8585)

> Wolf Creek Inn State Heritage Site
> 100 Front Street
> Wolf Creek, OR 97497
> 541-866-2474
> wolfcreek.inn@oregon.gov

Driving Directions: From the I-5 South onramp in Glendale, proceed south on I-5 to Exit 76. Take this exit and continue south on Old State Hwy 99 S for 0.3 miles to the Wolf Creek Inn, on your right.

☐ **Next Stop**: Wolf Creek Wildland Press

Right next to Ricki's Place, you'll find the small Wolf Creek Wildland Press. Look in the windows to see antique printing presses and guillotines from the 1800s, which are still in use today producing high quality printed materials, packaging, and works of art *by hand* for businesses large and small. Stop by for a visit, and if he has time, Blossom will be happy to tell you about the latest printing projects he's working on.

☐ **Next Stop**: Golden, OR – An Oregon Ghost Town

Located a little over 3 miles east of the Wolf Creek Tavern is the abandoned mining town of Golden, one of the finest examples of a ghost town in Oregon. Initially a home to gold miners working claims in the area during the mid-1800s, it grew over time and became an established town with approximately 100 people in 1890. Today, four structures managed by the Oregon State Parks & Recreation department are all that remain, including a school, a shed, a large church, and a building which used to house a post office and mercantile. Being a state park, visitors are welcome to visit and walk though the buildings.

Driving Directions: From the Wolf Creek Inn, continue south on Old State Hwy 99 S, the main road in front of the inn, for 0.3 miles and turn left / east to pass under I-5. After passing under I-5, continue to Coyote Creek Road and follow this 3.5 miles to Golden, OR and the Golden State Heritage Site.

☐ **Next Stop**: The Applegate Trail Interpretive Center

Early pioneers to Oregon traveled the Oregon Trail down the Columbia River or around the southern flanks of Mt. Hood, an arduous journey which was extremely dangerous. In 1846, members of the Applegate family set out to find a new route to Oregon, one which would run much further south. They were successful in their endeavor, establishing what would come to be known as The Applegate Trail.

Visit the Applegate Trail Interpretive Center to learn about the trail and its daily rigors, the important discovery of gold in the area, the emergence of the railroad, and much more.

Applegate Trail Interpretive Center
500 Sunny Valley Loop
Wolf Creek, OR 97497
541-476-8942

- Hours: Thursday - 10:30 a.m. to 4:30 p.m. - Friday, Saturday and Sunday - 12:00 p.m. to 4:30 p.m., spring through mid-October.

Driving Directions: From Golden, OR, return west, back to I-5 via Coyote Creek Road, and take I-5 south to Exit 71. Turn left / east onto Sunny Valley Loop and continue 0.4 miles to the Applegate Trail Interpretive Center on your right.

www.Discover-Oregon.com

☐ **Next Stop**: Grave Creek Covered Bridge

Immediately north of the Applegate Trail Interpretive Center is the Grave Creek Covered Bridge. Stop here and read the large interpretive sign at the south entrance to learn about the history of the bridge and how it got its name.

Driving Directions: The Grave Creek Covered Bridge is immediately north of the Applegate Trail Interpretive Center.

☐ **Next Stop**: Pottsville Historical Museum

Founded by Eugene "Debbs" Potts, Pottsville is home to over 1,000 historical items showcasing Oregon's history, with much of it outside, including old tractors, steam rollers, stage coaches, logging equipment, mining tools, and much more.

Pottsville also hosts numerous events throughout the year, including Father's Day weekend activities, an antique tractor show and pull, Southern Oregon's largest flea market, the Pottsville Pow Wow, the Rat-O-Rama Car Show, and more. Visit their web site to see if an event will be occurring while you're making a visit.

Pottsville Historical Museum
2400 Pleasant Valley Rd.
Merlin, OR 97532
541-476-7319
www.PottsvilleOregon.com

- Outdoor Exhibits Open: Daily – 10:00 a.m. – 6:00 p.m.
- Tours of the museums and pioneer town by appointment.

Driving Directions: From the Applegate Trail Interpretive Center, return to I-5 and drive south on I-5 for 5 miles to Exit 66. Take this exit and turn right / west onto Monument Drive. Continue south for 2.2 miles to Pleasant Valley Rd. Turn right / west onto Pleasant Valley Road and proceed 0.2 miles to the turn for the Pottsville Historical Museum.

www.Discover-Oregon.com

TONIGHT'S LODGING - THE WEASKU INN

It's hard to decide what is best about the Weasku Inn. Is it the friendly staff? The warm chocolate chip cookies awaiting guests in the evening? Perhaps it's the well-appointed rooms with comfortable beds? Or maybe it's that welcome feeling you get when you open the large wooden door and walk into the cozy lobby while nostalgic music softly plays.

You'll definitely enjoy your stay at the Weasku Inn. Built in 1924 near the banks of the Rogue River, the inn welcomes guests with 5 Lodge Rooms, 11 River Front Cabins, 1 A-Frame Cabin and a 3-bedroom River House.

Important: You will be making reservations at the Weasku Inn for **1 *or* 2 nights,** depending upon how you decide to go home. **Please read the information on Page 148 before making your reservations at The Weasku Inn.**

The Weasku Inn
5560 Rogue River Hwy
Grants Pass, OR 97527
541-471-8000

- Check-in: 3:00 p.m.
- Check-out: 12:00 Noon.
- 72 Hour cancellation policy.
- Children 12 and under stay free with an adult.
- The lodge and its accommodations are all non-smoking.
- No pets are allowed.
- Complimentary wireless Internet is available.
- Each room comes with a complimentary breakfast, afternoon hors d'oeuvres and evening milk & cookies.
- Some rooms come with fireplaces, Jacuzzi tubs, or balconies.
- An outdoor fire pit is available.
- Gluten free cookies are available upon request.

Note: If you're having trouble pronouncing the name, just ask about its history. You'll be surprised at how simple the story is, and once explained, you'll never forget it.

Driving Directions: From the Pottsville Historical Museum, return to Monument Drive and turn right / south. Continue for 3.8 miles to where Monument Drive merges with I-5 south. Continue south on I-5 for approximately 5 miles to Exit 55. From the exit, turn right / southeast onto Hwy 199 and follow this 2.1 miles to Hwy 99 / Rogue River Hwy. Turn left / east onto the Rogue River Hwy and follow this for 5 miles to the Weasku Inn on your left.

Notes

Day Seven

Oregon Caves National Monument & Preserve

DAY 7
GRANTS PASS TO THE OREGON CAVES NATIONAL MONUMENT & PRESERVE

Day 7 – Date: /   /

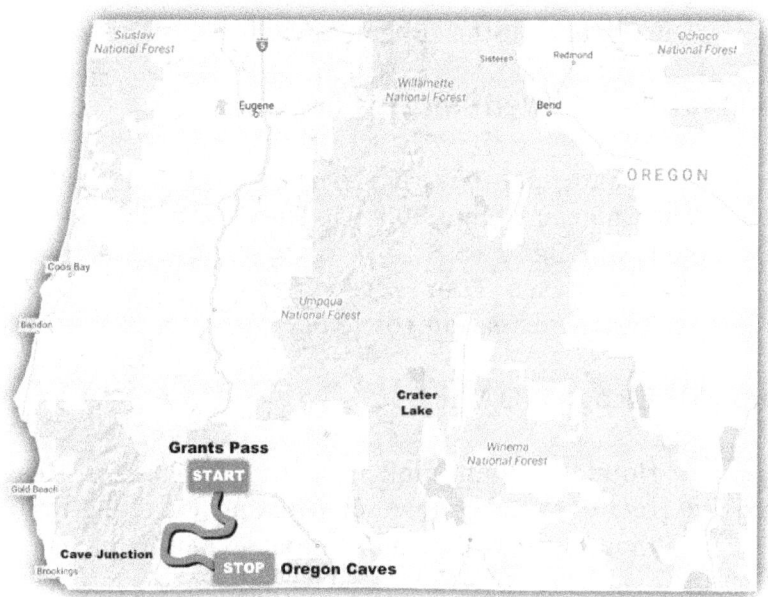

Summary: Where You're Going Today

- Williams, OR
- Kerby, OR
- Cave Junction, OR
- Oregon Caves National Monument & Preserve

Today is filled with highs and lows. You'll climb a road high above Williams, OR to enjoy a scenic vista overlooking much of Southwest Oregon, complete with the mountains surrounding Crater Lake in the far distance, before making your way to the Oregon Caves National Monument & Preserve, where you'll journey deep underground as part of a unique Oregon adventure. You'll finish the day by spending the night at the historic Chateau at the Oregon Caves.

Note: Before you begin, read the information about the tour times and wait times of The Oregon Caves, beginning on Page 133, so as to know how to allot your time throughout your day.

Tonight's Lodging:

- The Chateau at the Oregon Caves

Reservations Needed for This Segment:

- The Chateau at the Oregon Caves - 541-592-3400
- The Chateau Dining Room at The Oregon Caves - 541-592-3400
- Oregon Caves Tour Reservations - 877-444-6777 or visit www.recreation.gov

Today's Mileage: 83 Miles

Note: Fill your tank in Grants Pass before leaving today, or in the town of Williams, OR along the way, though gas will be more expensive in Williams.

Start

You'll begin the day by driving south out of Grants Pass on Hwy 238 / Williams Highway before turning towards the small town of Williams, OR. From here, you'll travel west on a narrow yet well-paved Forest Service road, which will take you up and over the mountains to Selma, OR and I-5. Next, you're continuing south on I-5 to the Oregon Caves, where you'll explore the wonders of underground Oregon before staying the night at the historic Chateau at the Oregon Caves.

☐ **First Stop**: Williams General Store

You may want a snack for today's drive, and there's no better place to stop than at the General Store in Williams, Oregon. Located at 1,375' in elevation, as the front façade tells you, it's a busy and well kept store welcoming all travelers. The husband and wife owners traded their corporate jobs to open the store in July 2016, worried that they may end up spending their time "watching dust bunnies make their way across the floor", but have since created a local destination that was quite busy on the morning we stopped in.

Note: There is gas here, as well as just a bit further down the road.

> Williams General Store
> 20180 Williams Hwy
> Williams, OR 97544
> 541-846-6212

Driving Directions: From the Weasku Inn, return west for 5 miles on Hwy 99 / Rogue River Highway to the interchange with Hwy 199 and Hwy 238. Turn left / southeast onto Hwy 199 and proceed for 0.1 mile to the intersection with Hwy 238, which leads to Murphy, OR and Jacksonville, OR. Turn left / south here and proceed 11.7 miles to where you'll continue straight onto Water Gap Road. Follow this for 5.8 miles to the Williams General Store on your right.

www.Discover-Oregon.com

☐ **Next Stop**: Cedar Flat Road Viewpoint

Shared with us by locals at the Williams General Store, this next stop offers plenty of scenery for your *scenic backroads and byways* journey.

Traveling through Williams, you'll veer right onto Cedar Flat Road and follow this west out of town, with the road soon turning into a narrow paved Forest Service road in good condition. Approximately 10 miles from Williams, you'll notice a large pullout with a gravel road to your right. Parking here, you can enjoy a tremendous view looking northeast over the Rogue Valley towards the mountains that hold Crater Lake in the far distance.

Note: Because of the higher elevation here, the road is usually closed by snow during the winter, but is typically open by Memorial Day in May, and oftentimes sooner. To get the snow status on this road, call the Williams General Store at 541-846-6212 or ask about it when you stop in. *Do not attempt to drive through the snow if the road is covered, even partially.* Instead, return north on Hwy 238 from Williams, OR to Hwy 199, and then proceed south on Hwy 199 to Selma, OR.

Driving Directions: Reset your odometer. From the Williams General Store, turn right / southeast onto Williams Hwy for 1 mile into Williams, OR. Veer right onto Cedar Flat Rd. and follow this for 4.7 miles from the Williams General Store to where it curves left while reducing down to a paved one lane Forest Service Road. Follow this to a little over 10 miles from the General Store to the viewpoint on your right in a clear cut.

Your next destination is Selma, OR, which is approximately 31 miles from the Williams General Store via Cedar Flat Road.

☐ **Next Stop**: Eight Dollar Mountain Botanical Wayside

As you make your way south on Hwy 199, you'll see a sign for the Eight Dollar Mountain Botanical Wayside. Stop here and make your way along a raised wheelchair accessible boardwalk through a unique Oregon botanical site offering uncommon wild plants and flowers that grow in abundance here. Fed by a small spring, you'll find the fuzzy-fringed petals of small Mariposa Lilies, fragrant white Wild Azaleas, and, in season, hundreds of Darlingtonia Californica, also known at Cobra Lilies, which are rare insect-eating plants. There are many other plants and wildflowers here, as well, many of which are explained on the interpretive signs along the trail.

- Open year-round
- Restrooms are located at the larger of two parking areas
- DO NOT pick any of the wildflowers
- Watch for ticks, poison oak and rattlesnakes, though it is highly unlikely you'll run into any of these while on the boardwalk itself.

Driving Directions: From the Cedar Flat Road Viewpoint, continue west on the paved Forest Service road until it becomes Deer Creek Rd., and follow this west into Selma, OR, approximately 31 miles from the Williams General Store. From Selma, drive south on Hwy 199 / Redwood Hwy for approximately 3.5 miles to Eight Dollar Road / FS 4201. Turn right / west here and look for the parking area for the botanical walk on your left in 1 mile. Park and walk up the steep paved drive across the road to find the boardwalk trailhead.

☐ **Next Stop**: The "It's a Burl" Gallery

One of the things we like about these road trips is stopping in places we usually pass by and leaving pleasantly surprised. "It's a Burl" Gallery fits into this category. We were amazed at the works of art carved from beautiful burl wood, and you will be, too. As a road cyclist, their bicycle created entirely out of wood was something to behold. Stop in on your way to the Kerbyville Historical Museum just down the road.

"It's a Burl" Gallery
24025 Redwood Hwy
Kerby, OR 97531
541-592-2141

- Open 7 days a week – 8:00 a.m. to 5:00 p.m.

Driving Directions: From the Eight Dollar Mountain Botanical Wayside, return to Hwy 199 and turn right / south. Continue for 2.3 miles to find the "It's a Burl" gallery on your left.

☐ **Next Stop**: Kerbyville Historical Museum

Stop in at the Kerbyville Historical Museum to see a well-curated display of over 50,000 items, large and small, tied to the recent history of the area, as well as the daily lives of Native Americans, pioneers, settlers, loggers and miners. In addition, you'll find an interesting display of WWII and Vietnam military items, as well as period-specific displays at the Naucke House next door, which was built in the 1880s.

> Kerbyville Museum
> 24195 Redwood Hwy
> Kerby, OR 97531
> 541-592-5252

Hours:

- April 1st through September 30th
- Open Tuesday through Saturday - 11:00 a.m. to 3:00 p.m., Sundays - 12:00 p.m. to 3:00 p.m.
- Admission: Adults: $6, Seniors: $4, Ages 6 to 16: $2, Children 5 and under are free. *Cash or check only.*

Driving Directions: The Kerbyville Historical Museum is located only a short distance south of the "It's a Burl" gallery.

☐ **Next Stop**: Oregon Caves National Monument & Preserve

Journey deep beneath the Siskiyou Mountains to explore a treasured Oregon icon...the Oregon Caves. A winding labyrinth of passages and great rooms totaling 15,000 linear feet, the caves present a rare and near endless display of marble in a multitude of colors and formations, including stalagmites, stalactites, columns, crystals, fossils and more.

We recommend taking a fascinating Ranger-guided interpretive tour to learn about these "Marble Halls of Oregon" and how they were formed, eventually discovered, and today protected.

Above ground, you can hike several different trails, see the "Big Tree", the largest diameter Douglas Fir in Oregon, have lunch at the grand 1934 Oregon Caves Chateau, and more.

> Oregon Caves National Monument and Preserve
> 19000 Caves Hwy
> Cave Junction, OR 97523
> 541-592-2100

Entrance Fees:

> There is no fee to enter the Oregon Caves National Monument & Preserve. There is a fee for tours, however.

Oregon Cave Tours:

- Discover Tour / General Tour - A 90 minute guided tour through the wonders of the Oregon Caves. - This tour involves 500 steps, and children must be at least 42" tall to participate.

- Candlelight Cave Tours - A 60 minute guided tour lit only by candlelight. - Open to explorers 10 and older.

All tours are led by a Ranger, who will act as your interpretive guide.

- Adult - 16 and Over: $10.00
- Youth - 15 and Under: $7.00
- Candlelight Tours: $10.00 - Ages 10 and over

Cave Tour Reservations:

> Reservations are highly recommended, especially from mid-May through Labor Day weekend. Make your reservations by calling 877-444-6777 or by visiting www.recreation.gov.

Tours are also available without reservations, on a first-come, first-served basis, but wait times during the summer months can often be up to 2 hours. It is recommended that you arrive before 12:00 noon to avoid long wait times, and before 2:00 p.m. to avoid sell outs of the tours. Sell outs often occur during the summer season, from mid-May through Labor Day weekend.

It is also recommended that you arrive one hour before your intended tour departure time. You will want to bring warm clothing, as the cave is a cool 44 degrees year-round. Also wear closed-toe shoes. Do not wear flip-flops, sandals or open-toe shoes. No flashlights, backpacks, large purses or tripods are allowed within the caves. In addition, pets are not allowed, and children may not be carried. All children must be at least 42" tall to participate in the tours.

Special note: Please leave your pets behind, as the parking lot is hot and offers no shaded parking. If you must board your pet, you may do so at Dr. Joe's Pet Hospital at 369 Caves Hwy, Cave Junction. 541-592-4589. Also available is Big Spring Boarding Kennels, 32225 Redwood Hwy., (6 Miles south of Caves Hwy) 541-596-2137.

Monument & Tour Hours: Tours occur roughly every ½ hour in the spring and fall months, and every 45 minutes in the summer, though these times can vary.

- **Spring** – Late March through mid-May – 9:30 a.m. – 4:00 p.m. - Thursday through Monday - (Closed Tuesday and Wednesday each week)
- **Summer** – Mid-May through early September – Monday through Sunday – 8:30 a.m. – 6:00 p.m.
- **Fall** – Early September through early November – 9:30 a.m. – 4:00 p.m.- Monday through Sunday
- **Winter**: - The caves are closed from early/mid-November through late March.

Photos courtesy of the National Park Service

Driving Directions: From the Kirbyville Museum, proceed south on Hwy 199 for approximately 2.5 miles to Cave Junction, OR and the intersection with Hwy 46 / Oregon Caves Highway. Turn left / east here and follow Hwy 46 for 20 miles to the Oregon Caves Monument and Preserve. This drive takes approximately 45 minutes. From the Oregon Caves parking lot, walk 900' to the Visitor Center to arrange for your tour.

Travel Trailers & Large RVs

Travel Trailers and large RVs are not recommended beyond Mile Post 12 / Grayback Campground on Hwy 46 to the Oregon Caves due to the winding nature of the road.

According to the Oregon Caves web site...If you have a large RV or travel trailer, park it (for free) at the Illinois Valley Visitor Center (IVVC) in Cave Junction which is located on Hwy 46 at 201 Caves Highway, Cave Junction, OR 97523. This is just a short distance from Hwy 199 intersection in Cave Junction. Call (541) 592-4076 for more information. Please be advised that the IVVC is not staffed after 4:30 pm. **Parking is at your own risk. It is recommended that you DO NOT park after hours and/or overnight.**

There are also two campgrounds located on Highway 46 that will accommodate recreational vehicles and trailers overnight. These are Country Hills Resort (privately owned, located at Mile 8 on Highway 46, eight miles southeast of Cave Junction) and Grayback Campground (a National Forest campground, located on Highway 46, twelve miles southeast of Cave Junction).

Country Hills Resort	Grayback Campground
7901 Caves Hwy	12000 Hwy 46
Cave Junction, OR 97523	Cave Junction, OR 97523
541-592-3406	541-592-4000

www.Discover-Oregon.com

TONIGHT'S LODGING - THE CHATEAU AT THE OREGON CAVES

Though not in a National Park, The Chateau at the Oregon Caves gives travelers the opportunity to stay in a National Park Lodge similar to the grand style of Crater Lake Lodge and Mt. Hood's majestic Timberline Lodge.

Constructed of massive old-growth wood beams finished with local materials, including Madrone, Cedar, Oak, Pine, and California Redwood, the six story Chateau at the Oregon Caves takes visitors back to the 1930s with its Arts and Crafts style furnishings, massive marble fireplace, wrought iron and brass lighting, and Italian stonework carved during President Roosevelt's CCC program.

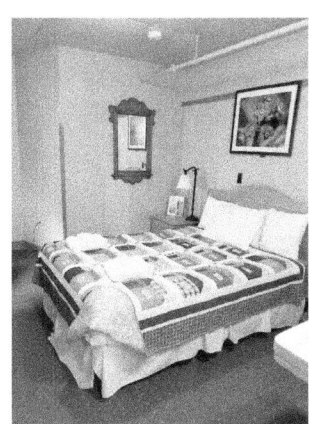

Deluxe Room with Monterey Style Furniture

Travelers will find simple, clean and well-appointed deluxe rooms, suites, standard and economy rooms, including some with beautiful views, as well as the Chateau Dining Room serving locally sourced northwest cuisine and award-winning Rogue Valley wines. The Chateau Dining Room is open from early May through early November, and reservations are highly recommended. Reservations may be made by calling 541-592-3400. Meals are also available at the Cave's Café, Gallery Deli, and the coffee shop.

>The Chateau at the Oregon Caves
>20000 Caves Hwy
>Cave Junction, OR 97523
>541-592-3400

Driving Directions: From Cave Junction, OR and the intersection with Hwy 46 / Oregon Caves Highway, follow Hwy 46 east for 20 miles to the Oregon Caves Monument and Preserve. This drive takes approximately 45 minutes. The Chateau at the Oregon Caves is located at the Oregon Caves National Monument, across from the Visitor Center.

www.Discover-Oregon.com

Notes

Day Eight

Jetboating on the Wild and Scenic Rogue River

Day 8
Jetboating on the Wild and Scenic Rogue River

Day 8 – Date: /   /

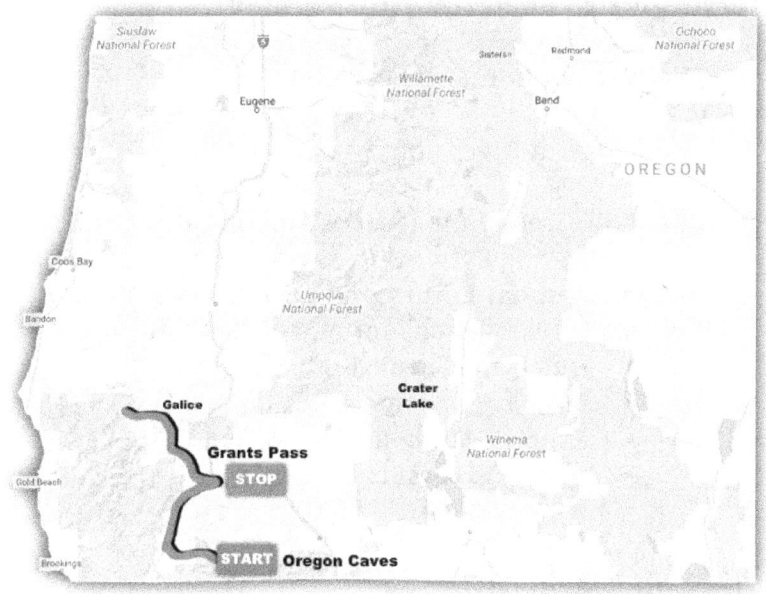

Summary: Where You're Going Today

- Rogue River Hellgate Jetboat Excursions

Today, your Oregon road trip ends on an exciting high note! You'll wake up at The Chateau at The Oregon Caves before driving back north to Grants Pass, OR and choosing from five different Hellgate jetboat excursions, each taking you through stunning rock canyons at over 40 mph on the scenic Rogue River. It's a true taste of Oregon summer fun! Afterwards, you can choose to head directly home or stay one more night at a nearby historic Oregon hotel before finishing your trip.

Tonight's Lodging:

- The Weasku Inn – Stay another night at the Weasku Inn, or choose to stay at The Lodge at Riverside or The Wolf Creek Inn. See Page 148 for additional information about how to make tonight's reservation.

Today's Mileage: 50 Miles

Reservations Needed for This Segment:

- **The Weasku Inn**: 541-471-8000
  or
- **The Lodge at Riverside**: 541-955-0600
  or
- **The Wolf Creek Inn**: Reserve America at 800-452-5687

- **Hellgate Jetboat Excursions** – 800-648-4874
  - Make reservations for one of the following:
    - Quick and Scenic Excursion
    - Brunch Excursion
    - Lunch Excursion
    - Dinner Excursion
    - Whitewater Adventure

Before You Leave:

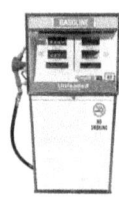 Fill your gas tank in Cave Junction, OR.

☐ **Today's Stop**: Rogue River Hellgate Jetboat Excursions

Imagine flying atop a scenic Oregon river at over 40 mph with 100' high rock walls whipping by so close to the boat that you're sure you could reach out and touch them. Breaking out into an open stretch of water, your guide hits the gas as the boat begins to dive left, suddenly careening into a 180 degree spin, followed by a huge splash of water...and everybody aboard bursting into laughter and applause.

A jetboat excursion on the wild and scenic Rogue River is just the way to wrap up your Southwest Oregon road trip. Choose from a menu of five family-friendly trips, all with a knowledgeable and skilled river guide who will provide a narrated overview of the river, its plentiful flora and fauna, the impressive geologic features you'll pass through, and stories about famous movies shot on the river itself, all with a boatload of thrills and laughs along the way.

Note: Departure times can vary depending upon river conditions, so *it is highly recommended that you call at least one day in advance to confirm your desired departure time.*

Note: A handful of trips stop at the OK Corral, a lodge overlooking the Rogue River and for exclusive use by Hellgate guests. Meals here are included in the price of your ticket.

Season: May 1st through mid-September

Tours: (Prices subject to change)

1. **Quick and Scenic Excursion** - $46.50 - $51

    A 2 hour, 36-mile round trip through Hellgate Canyon – No stops are included.

    Departure Times:
    - May: 1:45 p.m.
    - June through September: Twice daily - 8:45 a.m. and 1:45 p.m. - Late season afternoon departures may leave at 12:45 p.m.

2. **Brunch Excursion** - $44 - $67

    A 4 hour, 36-mile excursion – Includes a stop at Hellgate's exclusive OK Corral lodge for a champagne brunch.

    Departure Times:
    - Saturday and Sunday Only
    - May through September: 9:45 a.m.

3. **Lunch Excursion** - $41.50 - $61.50

    A 3.5 hour, 36-mile excursion – Includes a stop at Hellgate's exclusive OK Corral for a delicious country-style lunch.

Departure Times:
- Monday through Friday Only
- May through September: 9:30 a.m.

4. **Dinner Excursion** - $47.50 - $75

   A 4 hour 36-mile excursion – Includes a stop at Hellgate's exclusive OK Corral for an all-you-can-eat dinner.

   Departure Times:
   - May through September
   - 4:00 p.m. until mid-August, then 3:00 p.m.

5. **Whitewater Adventure** - $51.50 - $74

   A 5 hour, 75-mile excursion – Journey deep downriver on the Rogue while you experience more rapids, dramatic scenery, and Oregon wildlife. Stop for a meal at the beautiful Morrison's Lodge along the way. Note that the price of your meal at the lodge is not included with your ticket, as it is with the other jetboat excursions.

   Departure Times:
   - May through September, though dependent upon water levels late in the season
   - 8:30 a.m. and 2:45 p.m.

Plan to arrive and check in at least 15 minutes prior to your departure time. *Your travel time between the Oregon Caves National Monument and Hellgate Jetboat Excursions will be approximately 1.5 hours.* (48 Miles) Keep in mind that you could find yourself behind a slow moving vehicle during part of this drive, so it may take longer.

What to Wear:

During the spring season of May through early June, when the weather is less stable and the water is cooler, and the month of September, when it is cooler out in the afternoons and evenings, it is wise to dress in layers and bring a water-resistant or waterproof coat and pair of pants, or a lightweight rain poncho, in case you feel you need it. Note that it is always cooler during the early morning hours and when you're returning from the dinner trip.

During the summer months, you can expect highs in the 80s and 90s, so typical summer attire, including shorts, t-shirts and sports sandals, is fine. *Be sure to bring sunscreen, sunglasses and water*, and a hat is advised, since you'll be in the sun for much of your trip.

It is recommended that, for your post-excursion comfort, you have an extra set of clothes available in your car if you are making an extended ride back home or to your hotel.

Note that bathing suits are not considered appropriate attire for dining at the OK Corral.

We have found it beneficial to bring a small pair of binoculars for viewing wildlife while on the jetboat excursion, but they are not necessary.

For more information about a Rogue River Hellgate Jetboat Excursion, visit the FAQ page at www.Hellgate.com.

> Rogue River Hellgate Jetboat Excursions
> 966 SW 6th Street
> Grants Pass, OR 97526
> 541-479-7204

Driving Directions: From the Oregon Caves National Monument, return 20 miles on Hwy 46 to Cave Junction. Turn right / north here and follow Hwy 199 back to Grants Pass for approximately 28 miles to the exit for Hwy 99 North / City Center. Follow this exit onto Hwy 99 / SE 7th Street and turn left / west in 0.7 miles onto SE Voorhies Way. In 1 block, turn left / south onto SE 6th St., where you'll find Hellgate Jetboat Excursions on your right.

Notes

Tonight's Lodging - Your Choice of 3 Locations or Going Home

You have four choices for tonight's lodging, the first three of which mean your trip isn't over quite yet!

Options #1, 2 & 3: After your Rogue River jetboat excursion, spend another night at a nearby hotel and begin your trip home tomorrow, on the morning of Day 9. We recommend making reservations for this evening at one of the following:

- **The Weasku Inn** – 541-471-8000 - If you choose to spend another night at The Weasku Inn, then you'll need to make reservations for the night of Day 6 and tonight, Day 8, when making your initial reservations for Day 6. See Page 108.

- **The Lodge at Riverside** – 541-955-0600 – Located at 955 SE 7th Street, Grants Pass, OR 97526, the nicely appointed Lodge at Riverside is conveniently located only a couple of blocks east from Hellgate Jetboat Excursions.

- **The Wolf Creek Inn and Tavern** – Travel back north approximately 21 miles and stay at the historic Wolf Creek Inn and Tavern, which you toured on Day 6. Recall, however, that the inn does not serve meals, but the family friendly Ricki's Place restaurant is next door. Reservations for the inn may be made via Reserve America at 800-452-5687.

Option #4: Finish your Rogue River jetboat excursion and, depending upon which tour you took, drive home that afternoon or evening, provided you live nearby.

Before You Leave:

Fill your gas tank in Grants Pass.

www.Discover-Oregon.com

Phone Numbers - Oregon Road Trips - Southwest Edition

- Cottage Grove Ranger District Office: 541-767-5000
  - cgrdinfo@fs.fed.us
- Crater Lake Lodge Reservations
  - Crater Lake Lodge Reservations: For 1 to 2 days in advance - 541-594-2255 - xt 3200
  - Crater Lake Lodge Reservations: More than 2 days in advance - 888-774-2728
- Crater Lake National Park:
  - General Information: 541-594-3000
  - Boat Tours Information: 541-594-3000
  - Boat Tours Reservations: 888-774-2728
  - Lodging Information: 541-594-3000
  - Road Conditions: 541-594-3000 - #0
- Crater Lake Trolley: 541-882-1896
- Harry & David Tour: 877-322-8000
- Hellgate Jetboat Excursions: 541-479-7204
- Historic Ashland Springs Hotel - 541-488-1700
- Jacksonville Trolley: 541-899-8118
- Les Schwab Tire Center - Eugene: 541-485-2822
- Les Schwab Tire Center - Grants Pass: 541-955-5200
- Les Schwab Tire Center - Klamath Falls: 541-882-6623
- Les Schwab Tire Center - Medford: 541-772-5744
- Les Schwab Tire Center - Myrtle Creek: 541-863-5251
- Les Schwab Tire Center - Roseburg: 541-672-6745
- Oregon Caves National Monument: 541-592-2100
- Oregon Caves Tour Reservations: 877-444-6777
- Segways of Jacksonville: 541-899-5269
- Steamboat Inn & Dinner Reservations: 541-498-2230
- The Chateau at the Oregon Caves: 541-592-3400
- The Lodge at Riverside - Grants Pass: 541-955-0600
- The Weasku Inn: 541-471-8000
- The Wolf Creek Inn: Via Reserve America - 800-452-5687
- The Wood House: 541-826-2177

Your Next Oregon Road Trip Is Ready!

Oregon Road Trips - Northeast Edition

Just as with this guide to Southwest Oregon, we've already laid out an exciting 9-day journey through Northeast Oregon's scenic backroads and byways for you. Along the way, you'll ride aboard a historic steam train, wander Oregon ghost towns, ascend in a cable tram to over 8,000', stay at the 1907 Balch Hotel, board the Sumpter Valley Dredge, explore Cottonwood Canyon, ride the rails on a 2-seater, explore unique shops, eat at great restaurants, meet friendly people and so much more!

Your next road trip awaits, and it's already planned for you!

Available Now at Retailers Throughout Oregon and Online

AND ANOTHER GREAT ROAD TRIP IS READY!

Oregon Road Trips - Southeast Edition

Just like with this Southwest edition, you'll simply turn each page as you motor along and choose which points of interest to stop at and explore during your day's journey, *all while making your way toward that evening's stay at a historic Oregon hotel.*

During your 7 to 9-day road trip, you'll drive to the top of 9,734' Steens Mountain, stay in the 1923 Frenchglen Hotel, explore the remote Leslie Gulch, see how stage coaches are built, dig for fossils, hike "Crack in the Ground", look for wild Mustangs, eat at a truly unique Oregon restaurant, marvel at the geologic wonders of the Journey Through Time Scenic Byway and so much more!

**Available Now at Retailers
Throughout Oregon and Online**

Now Enjoy An Oregon Coast Road Trip!

Oregon Road Trips – Oregon Coast Edition

Pack your bags, because you're about to explore the grandeur of Oregon's dramatic coastline during an adventurous 9-day road trip from Astoria south to Brookings. You'll journey along Oregon's beautiful Highway 101 as you discover countless scenic beaches, tour historic lighthouses, wander through quaint beach towns, watch whales spouting just off shore, ride in the cab of a 1925 steam locomotive, eat tasty Dungeness Crab fresh off the boat...or catch your own, stay in historic hotels, explore unique shops, meet friendly people and so much more!

Your perfect Oregon Coast road trip awaits!

Available Now at Retailers Throughout Oregon and Online

DISCOVER THE COLUMBIA RIVER GORGE!

Oregon Road Trips – Columbia River Gorge Edition

Journey along the Historic Columbia River Highway deep into the Columbia River Gorge, where you'll spend 5 days seeing the Gorge's majestic waterfalls, flying in a vintage 2-seater biplane, hiking through the historic Mosier Tunnels, stepping into the void on an exciting zip line tour, walking amidst the Gorge's beautiful spring wildflowers, finding your next book at Oregon's oldest bookstore, and even spotting Giraffes, Zebras, Camels, Ostriches and more!

Your perfect Columbia River Gorge road trip awaits, and it's already planned for you!

Available Now at Retailers Throughout Oregon and Online

Road Trip Oregon's Majestic Mt. Hood!

Oregon Road Trips – Mt. Hood Edition

An alpine Oregon Road Trip adventure is waiting for you!

Set out on an exciting Oregon road trip where every night ends at a charming historic hotel, finishing with majestic Timberline Lodge at 6,000' on the south shoulder of Mt. Hood! Explore the Historic Columbia River Highway, hike the unique Mosier Tunnels route, visit Oregon's oldest bookstore, walk among the Columbia River Gorge's colorful spring wildflowers, fly in a vintage 2-seater biplane, ride to over 7,000' on the Magic Mile Chairlift, discover the rustic and remote 1889 Cloud Cap Inn on Mt. Hood's eastern flank, and so much more.

Available Now at Retailers Throughout Oregon, Discover-Oregon.com and Online

What to See, Do & Explore on the Oregon Coast!

At 363 miles long, Oregon's scenic coastline is filled with countless natural wonders and attractions to see, do, and explore. Hike to a high bluff to watch for whales, walk a long sandy beach, explore a historic lighthouse, catch a live Dungeness crab, join in the fun of a sandcastle building contest, even ride aboard an old-fashioned steam train. The problem is...how do you uncover all of these activities to get the most out of your trip? The solution is the new *Oregon Coast Guide*. Inside these pages, you'll discover over 200 fun and adventurous things to see, do and explore while visiting the Oregon Coast, complete with descriptions, photos, maps, tips, a whale watching guide and much more.

Available Now at Retailers Throughout Oregon, Discover-Oregon.com and Online

EXPLORE THE COLUMBIA RIVER GORGE

Cutting a deep gorge between Oregon and Washington, the majestic Columbia River Gorge is filled with scenic vistas, graceful waterfalls, amazing attractions, captivating history, and countless adventures, and they are all waiting for you in the *Columbia River Gorge – An Explorer's Guide*. With this guide you'll discover the many waterfalls of "Waterfall Alley", walk among the gorge's colorful spring wildflowers, fly in a vintage 2-seater biplane over Mt. Hood, see over 300 restored antique motorcars and aeroplanes up close, explore the Hood River "Fruit Loop", hike classic gorge trails, visit Oregon's oldest bookstore, discover some great new cycling roads and routes, watch world-class sailboarding, see giraffes, zebras, camels, and bison, stay a night or two or three at one of the gorge's historic hotels, watch a master glass blower create a stunning trout out of glass, eat the biggest ice cream cone in your life, and so much more!

**Available Now at Retailers
Throughout Oregon and Online**

Discover Washington's Olympic Peninsula

Washington's Olympic Peninsula has always been somewhat of a mystery, but now it's an adventurous and perfectly planned 6-day road trip! Set out to discover this exciting world that varies from high alpine peaks and lofty hiking trails to long sandy beaches and captivating ocean vistas. Stay at and explore the busy Victorian seaport of Port Townsend, visit a historic lighthouse, tour a vintage airplane museum, kayak on the Strait of Juan de Fuca, see majestic orcas, humpbacks, and gray whales, sleep in your very own castle, stand in the quietest place in the United States, explore unique shops, eat at great restaurants, meet friendly people, and so much more!

Your perfect Northern Olympic Peninsula road trip awaits...and it's already planned for you!

**Available Now at Retailers
Throughout Washington and Online**

About the Authors

Mike & Kristy Westby at Oregon's Crater Lake NP

Having been to all six "corners" of Oregon...North, South, East, West, Top and Bottom, (The top of Mt. Hood and the Oregon Coast) we decided it would be fun to take off on a series of multi-day road trips throughout the state. During our travels, we were surprised at the number of folks we met along the way who said they've always wanted to do the same thing, but they didn't know where to even begin planning such a trip. How do you find interesting places? What routes do you take? How do separate it all into even days, all while ending each day at a historic hotel? With that in mind, we decided to write our road trip guides so other like-minded souls can easily benefit from the knowledge we've gleaned over the years and set out on their own adventures.

We'd love to hear about the journeys you've taken with our different road trip guides, so feel free to drop us a note anytime or send us a photo, especially if you're on the road!

ContactUs@Discover-Oregon.com

MIRIAM TULLER'S OREGON TRAIL EXPERIENCE

On Page 116, you read about the Tuller Family gravesite on the Cow Creek Scenic Byway. What follows is the personal account of Miriam Tuller and her journey westward to Oregon.

Miriam (Robinson-Thompson) Tuller's trail experience was recorded in the Oregon Pioneer Association Transactions, Number 23, 1895:

Crossing the Plains in 1845
By Mrs. Miriam A. Tuller, Glendale

I was born May 29, 1826, in Edwardsville, Madison County, Illinois; was married to Arthur H. Thompson, April 17th, 1844.

We started on March 22nd, 1845, from near Hennepin, Putnam County, Illinois, in the company with Eugene Skinner and wife, for Oregon; crossed the Illinois river there, and bid farewell to friends and acquaintances - my husband fired with patriotism to help keep the country from British rule, and I was possessed with a spirit of adventure and a desire to see what was new and strange. From Illinois River we went to Quincy; crossed the Mississippi River there and went to Lexington and crossed the Missouri at that place. From there to the state line, as it was then called, the place agreed upon for the emigrants to meet for a final start for Oregon; there we started from on May 11th, with a company of four hundred and eighty wagons, nearly all ox teams, and some large bands of loose cattle. That was a very dry, warm spring and thus far a very pleasant experience for me. Stephen Meek, a brother of the renowned Joe Meek, was elected guide. I was not acquainted with any one coming to Oregon when I started, except my husband, but I made many very agreeable acquaintances, many of whom I have always held in kind remembrance.

We were unable to make much headway with so large a company, so agreed to divide. Then we were in a company of eighty wagons and that was far too many; so kept separating, some times twenty wagons and often only four or five - that was more convenient - and we had become indifferent to fear. We traveled up Platte River and forded it. Then we went in the buffalo country; there were solid masses of these as far as the eye could reach, and we had fresh meat galore. The little, graceful antelopes were plenty and now and then we saw a big horn and an elk.

We stopped one day at Fort Laramie. From Platte we journeyed to Sweetwater, then to Green River, which we forded by placing blocks under the wagon bed to raise it up to keep things inside dry. We camped one day near Fort Bridger, then on to Fort Hall. Captain Grant, of the Hudson's Bay Company, was in charge; he gave us the consoling information that the Indians would kill us before we got to Oregon; but they proved better than represented. We had little trouble with Indians, but they stole some things. We saw thousands of them, many in the same style as Adam and Eve when first in the Garden of Eden. Next went to Fort Boise; Mr. Craig, of the Hudson's Bay Company, was in charge. He was more polite than Captain Grant; he only said we had better wait for more company, and he sent a French servant with a large canoe to take us women across Snake River, where we crossed it the second time. The men and teams forded it; then Bear River, Burnt River, Malheur and Powder Rivers, with their numerous Indian camps, were passed; the beautiful Blue Mountains, Grand Ronde Valley and river, then John Day's River and next DesChutes or Fall River. This we had to ferry, the first since leaving the Missouri. There was a sand storm raging; some Indians were there with their canoes who were more than willing to take us over for some calico shirts. The wagons were unloaded and taken apart and after many loads, we were safely over. The teams had to swim. Then we went to The Dalles; here Father Waller and another missionary were stationed, who sold us some beef and potatoes, for provisions were getting low.

There were a few row boats at The Dalles to take the emigrants down the Columbia and up the Willamette, as that was the only way to reach the Willamette Valley with wagons at that time. There were so many of us, although one-third of our number had turned off at Fort Hall to go to California under Wm. B. Ide, guided by the old trapper Greenwood, that it would take too long for all to go in those small boats, so some concluded to go through the Cascade Mountains. S.K. Barlow was the moving spirit in this undertaking. There was only an Indian trail that some stock had been driven over. We started with teams and wagons. We had overcome so many difficulties that we felt quite sure we could go almost anywhere. We got along quite well until we came to the heavy timber. The men worked on the road for about two weeks, but gave up hope of getting the wagons through that fall, as it was now October, and concluded it was best to send the women and children out of the mountains. I was mounted on a Cayuse pony and in company with Mr. and Mrs. Buffum and Captain Palmer, left husband and camp - everything - but a few clothes and a little provisions, to try to reach some place before the rain set in. The first night after we left camp rain commenced and it rained all the time until we got through the mountains. The trail that we traveled went up over the south side of Mt. Hood, away up to and over perpetual snow. The coming down was worse, the zigzag trail a foot or more deep with sand. We camped on the side of the mountain as night overtook us. There it rained very hard all night. We had no tent or shelter of any kind. The fourth night we met three men from Oregon City, coming to meet those emigrants in the mountains with some provisions, as they had heard we were in distress. We were not in any immediate danger of starving but the beef and sugar were very acceptable, and to be so kindly thought of by strangers was very cheering. The names of those men were Mathew Gilmore, Peter G. Stewart and Charles Gilmore. The provisions were contributed by the people around Oregon City.

There were many many fallen trees across the trail that the horses had to jump; the streams were deep, swift and cold. We reached Oregon City the sixth day from camp, but when I saw a woman on a very poor horse with a little child in her lap and one strapped on behind her and two or three tied on another horse, I felt very very thankful and imagined I was only having a picnic.

I found a pleasant place to stop and was very kindly treated by Mr. and Mrs. Holmes, near Oregon City. I remained there until February; then went to Yamhill County, where we stayed through the summer. In June my husband and others who had left their wagons in the mountains took their teams and returned to bring them out, as the road had been cleared of timber. The mice had made lint of most of my clothing and bedding, but I was glad to get what was left, as things of that kind were very scarce in Oregon at that time. The fall of 1846 my parents came, and we all went down the Columbia River, to Clatsop Plains.

In the fall of 1848, when gold was discovered in California my husband went, as did many others, to seek gold, but never returned. He was murdered by the Indians near Mormon Island on American River. There were four in camp and none left to tell the tale. Their names were Arthur H. Thompson, Talmage B. Wood, Robert Alexander and ___ English.

July 30th, 1850, I was married to Jeremiah G. Tuller. I lived in Clatsop County seven years and went to Benton County August, 1854, where I stayed until 1880. My present post office address is Glendale, Douglas County, Oregon. My maiden name was Robinson.

We Recommend...

Restore Oregon

As you journeyed through Southwest Oregon, you no doubt noticed the many historic structures which capture the history and culture of our state. Many, however, are in urgent need of protection. Restore Oregon is dedicated to "taking care of the places that make Oregon, OREGON" and preserving them for future generations. Learn more at RestoreOregon.org

Wildland Press - Wolf Creek, Oregon

At Wildland Press, printing is an art and a passion. Using antique presses from the 1800s, combined with modern technology mixed with old world skill, this unique print shop crafts by hand everything from simple business and social cards to complex wedding invitations and custom product packaging. Be it die cutting, laser carving or printing on materials a digital printer can't touch, including handmade paper, cloth, wood and even leather, Wildland Press is set up to turn your ideas into reality. Learn more at www.BlossomMerz.com

Les Schwab Tire Centers

If you're on the road and have a flat tire, brake issues or a similar problem, we highly recommend the very helpful folks at your nearby Les Schwab Tire Center.

Located throughout Oregon. Find phone numbers for multiple locations in Southwest Oregon on Page 150.

Antiques & Oddities

A Columbia River Gorge "destination" for over 25 years, Antiques & Oddities in Bingen, WA is home to an eclectic collection of quality antiques from near and far, including Asia and Europe.

211 W. Steuben St., Bingen, WA
509-493-4242

Are You a Disneyland Fan?

Enjoy three great books which reveal the hidden secrets and story elements that the Disney Imagineers have purposely hidden for park guests to find and enjoy; 1) *The Hidden Secrets & Stories of Disneyland*, 2) *Disneyland In-Depth*, and 3) *The Hidden Secrets & Stories of Walt Disney World*.

Available online and at the prestigious Walt Disney Family Museum.

The Great Unbaked Chocolate Factory & Unbakery

For a different artisan chocolate experience, choose The Great Unbaked Chocolate Factory. Handcrafted in Grants Pass, Oregon, these award-winning chocolates are made with the finest raw ingredients. Order and have some shipped to you today. www.TheGreatUnaked.com

Are You a Walt Disney World Fan?

See and experience Walt Disney World in an entirely new way! Written by Oregon author Mike Fox, *The Hidden Secrets & Stories of Walt Disney World* reveals over 300 of the fun secret story elements that the Disney Imagineers have hidden throughout all four parks.

Available online, as well as at the prestigious Walt Disney Family Museum and the Walt Disney Hometown Museum.

Camp Attitude

"Changing lives one camper at a time!"

Camp Attitude provides a welcoming camp experience for disabled youth and their families. Here, children with special needs can participate in all of the fun, games, excitement and interaction of a thrilling week-long "summer camp" experience, all for a nominal fee, thanks to donations from contributors who enjoy seeing a smile on a child's face...and a squirt gun in their hand!

Camp Attitude is a faith-based non-profit organization, and donations may be made by visiting their web site at www.CampAttitude.org

>Camp Attitude
>PO Box 2017
>45829 S Santiam Hwy
>Foster, OR 97345
>541-401-1052

www.ingramcontent.com/pod-product-compliance
Lightning Source LLC
Chambersburg PA
CBHW070603010526
44118CB00012B/1439